OSWorkflow

A guide for Java developers and architectsto integrating open-source Business Process Management

Diego Adrian Naya Lazo

PUBLISHING

BIRMINGHAM - MUMBAI

OSWorkflow

First published: August 2007

Production Reference: 1210807

Published by Packt Publishing Ltd.
32 Lincoln Road
Olton
Birmingham, B27 6PA, UK.

ISBN 978-1-847191-52-6

www.packtpub.com

Cover Image by Vinayak Chittar (vinayak.chittar@gmail.com)

Credits

Author

Diego Adrian Naya Lazo

Reviewers

Gabriel Bruno

Hani Suleiman

Juan Pedro Danculovic

Development Editor

Nanda Padmanabhan

Assistant Development Editor

Rashmi Phadnis

Technical Editors

Rashmi Phadnis

Saurabh Singh

Editorial Manager

Dipali Chittar

Project Manager

Patricia Weir

Project Coordinator

Abhijeet Deobhakta

Indexer

Mithil Kulkarni

Proofreader

Chris Smith

Production Coordinators

Manjiri Nadkarni

Shantanu Zagade

Cover Designer

Shantanu Zagade

About the Author

Diego Naya Lazo is a Chief Enterprise Architect living in Buenos Aires, Argentina. He currently works for Argentina's biggest healthcare provider and has more than 10 years of experience in the IT industry. He has participated in several projects as a hands-on software architect and performed the technical lead role in many companies. His interest in computer programming began with his desire to create the most vivid 3D animations as a graphic designer at the age of 15.

His interests range from Enterprise Architecture to SOA and BPM technology. He is a Sun Certified Enterprise Architect and holds other certifications such as: SCJP, SCWCD, MCSA, and Security+. He is also a member of the WWISA and GEAO enterprise architects' associations as well as an active developer of the OSWorkflow project. He holds a Bachelors degree in IT and is currently enrolled in an MBA program.

Away from work, Diego enjoys traveling all around the world with his family. You can reach him at `dienaya@gmail.com`.

I want to thank Gustavo Aguirre, my role model and mentor, for giving me advice and my reviewers Juan Pedro Danculovic and Gabriel Bruno, for loving this as much as I do. Hani Suleiman, for your commitment to the project and the whole OSWorkflow team.

This book is dedicated to Mariela and Mauro—You are the light that shines on my path through life.

About the Reviewers

Gabriel A. Bruno lives in Argentina and has been working since 1997 in the IT industry. Among his various activities are consulting services in many companies, mainly in the financial industry, and he also has performed activities as an instructor of OO analysis and design, and data structures.

In 1998 he discovered the open-source world through the GNU Linux operating system, which he adopted to perform his duties. Two years later, he began to use Java and subsequently the J2EE platform professionally.

He's currently working as a Java Architect for an important health insurance company in Argentina.

I greatly thank Diego Naya for including me in this endeavor.

Hani Suleiman is the CTO of Formicary, a company specializing in integration and portal solutions for financial firms. He also is an elected individual member of the JCP Executive Committee, as well as serving on a number of enterprise-related Expert Groups.

Juan Pedro Danculovic received his Computer Science Analyst degree at the UNLP-La Plata, Argentina in 2001.

He has researched in several areas such as object-oriented and web applications design, and also web personalization aspects in web services and applications.

He has also taught web application architecture aspects courses at the UNLP.

He is currently working in the IT Architecture department at the biggest health care services company in Argentina.

Table of Contents

Introduction

OSWorkflow is a Java-based open-source workflow engine. It helps you to focus your work on the business logic and rules rather than working on heavy coding. Integrating OSWorkflow into your application is very easy and fast. OSWorkflow provides all of the workflow constructs that you might come across in real-life processes like steps, conditions, loops, splits, joins, roles, etc. The latest version of OSWorkflow has a GUI for developing workflows, which simplifies creating workflows for simple needs. To get the best out of it, creating workflows by XML coding is recommended. OSWorkflow takes advantage of many existing Java open-source projects, including:

- BeanShell: For workflow scripting
- OpenForBusiness: Entity engine persistence support
- GLUE: For a SOAP interface
- Quartz: For job scheduling

OSWorkflow can work in any J2EE container, including servlet containers (EJB support does not work here). OSWorkflow was designed to be as flexible as possible to fit the needs of many unique requirements.

This book explains OSWorkflow, without assuming any prior knowledge of Business Process Management. Real-life examples are used to clarify concepts. It gives step-by-step instructions on how to do things. The basics are explained first and then examples help to clarify and reinforce the principles.

What This Book Covers

Chapter 1 gives an overview of the BPM technology and the workflow engine, along with an analysis of the different types of BPMS.

Chapter 2 introduces OSWorkflow and teaches the basics of the workflow engine along with a real-life example.

Chapter 3 introduces several key features of OSWorkflow like handling persistent and transient variables, variable interpolation, built-in OSWorkflow functions, Conditions, and BeanShell scripting.

Chapter 4 covers Persistence of variables across invocations, and the FunctionProviders along with integrating OSWorkflow with Spring.

Chapter 5 introduces and integrates Rules engine and Drools open-source rule engine.

In *Chapter 6* we explore the Quartz task scheduler and its integration with OSWorkflow and we give a tutorial with Quartz sending events and actions to OSWorkflow.

Chapter 7 introduces Event Stream Processing and Complex Event Processing. We give an OSWorkflow function provider that interfaces with the ESPer CEP engine and allows the monitoring of real-time process information and events.

Chapter 8 gives OSWorkflow visualization of its business process information with the Pentaho open-source BI solution. Using the charting capabilities of Pentaho we build an enterprise process dashboard to monitor and analyze the processes.

Who is This Book For

The book is aimed at experienced Java developers and system architects who want to develop complex Java applications using the OSWorkflow workflow engine. OSWorkflow is a flexible low-level workflow implementation for developers and architects; it is not a quick "plug-and-play" solution for non-technical end users.

Conventions

In this book, you will find a number of styles of text that distinguish between different kinds of information. Here are some examples of these styles, and an explanation of their meaning.

There are three styles for code. Code words in text are shown as follows: "The OSWorkflow descriptor XML must have a root element of `workflow` and obligatory child elements named `steps` and `initial-actions`."

A block of code will be set as follows:

```
...
<steps>
 <step id="1" name="Employee request">
  <actions>
  <action id="1" name="Request holidays">
   <results>
```

```
        <unconditional-result old-status="Finished" step="2"
                                              status="Requested"/>
      </results>
     </action>
    </actions>
  </step>
  ...
```

When we wish to draw your attention to a particular part of a code block, the relevant lines or items will be made bold:

```
<actions>
    <action id="1" name="Action 1">
      <results>
          <unconditional-result old-status="Finished" status=
                                       "Pending" split="1"/>
      </results>
    </action>
</actions>
```

New terms and **important words** are introduced in a bold-type font. Words that you see on the screen, in menus or dialog boxes for example, appear in our text like this: "You can simply click on the **Authors** link located on the books listing page in your browser."

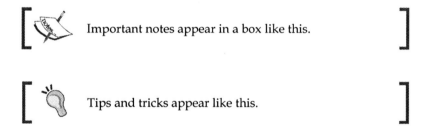

Important notes appear in a box like this.

Tips and tricks appear like this.

Reader Feedback

Feedback from our readers is always welcome. Let us know what you think about this book, what you liked or may have disliked. Reader feedback is important for us to develop titles that you really get the most out of.

To send us general feedback, simply drop an email to feedback@packtpub.com, making sure to mention the book title in the subject of your message.

If there is a book that you need and would like to see us publish, please send us a note in the **SUGGEST A TITLE** form on www.packtpub.com or email suggest@packtpub.com.

If there is a topic that you have expertise in and you are interested in either writing or contributing to a book, see our author guide on www.packtpub.com/authors.

Customer Support

Now that you are the proud owner of a Packt book, we have a number of things to help you to get the most from your purchase.

Downloading the Example Code for the Book

Visit http://www.packtpub.com/support, and select this book from the list of titles to download any example code or extra resources for this book. The files available for download will then be displayed.

The downloadable files contain instructions on how to use them.

Errata

Although we have taken every care to ensure the accuracy of our contents, mistakes do happen. If you find a mistake in one of our books—maybe a mistake in text or code—we would be grateful if you would report this to us. By doing this you can save other readers from frustration, and help to improve subsequent versions of this book. If you find any errata, report them by visiting http://www.packtpub.com/support, selecting your book, clicking on the **Submit Errata** link, and entering the details of your errata. Once your errata are verified, your submission will be accepted and the errata added to the list of existing errata. The existing errata can be viewed by selecting your title from http://www.packtpub.com/support.

Questions

You can contact us at questions@packtpub.com if you are having a problem with some aspect of the book, and we will do our best to address it.

1
BPM and Workflow Basics

This chapter gives an overview of the BPM technology and its core component, the workflow engine. We will analyze the different types of BPMS and the flexibility they provide in terms of workgroup collaboration and system orchestration. A brief outline of the topics covered in this chapter is as follows:

- Business Process Orientation
- What is a BPMS?
- Types of BPM Systems
- Components of a BPM solution
- Open-source BPMS

Business Process Orientation

Today's marketplace is more global and competitive than ever. Big players are trying to attract new clients along with maintaining the existing ones (thereby making more profit for shareholders), and smaller players are entering the markets with innovative products. To add to this, customers are demanding better prices and service and governments are continuously changing regulations.

Businesses redefine themselves in order to adapt to this environment or to create new market niches for exploitation. Technology plays an important role in realizing these changes and adaptations. With the appropriate technology and tools, businesses can reduce costs, raise margins, and make the most of the existing information to understand the clients better and thus create new markets based on this data.

Businesses are focusing on internal efficiency, which aims at realizing the goals of making profit, reducing costs, creating and maintaining customers, and negotiating with suppliers in faster, cheaper, and improved ways.

With the appropriate use of technology, businesses can benefit in many ways such as greater revenue, bigger margins, automated processes, improved decision making, and so on.

Every business has a set of connected activities and functions driven by business rules such as sales, account receivables, R & D, and so on. The daily operation of such essential processes costs a big chunk of revenue from shareholders. **Business Process Management (BPM)** technology promises continuous enhancement of the business processes.

To diminish these costs and maximize the profit generated, each business process must be efficient and smooth. The more visible these processes are, the more we can modify them to align with the organizational strategy.

Every corporate strategy and company mission wants to treat the customer in the best possible way it can, but are the customer service processes aligned with the strategy? Is the bureaucracy of my service as minimal as possible? Are my business processes impeding the efforts of employees to excel at customer support? Am I generating long-lasting bonds between my customers and my company?

These questions can only be answered by knowing the processes, the actors, the context, etc. Today's business executives are held accountable for the performance of the processes they manage. Accountability needs objective measures, and how can we measure what we don't know?

BPR and BPM

In the early nineties, a trend called **Business Process Reengineering (BPR)** emerged as a panacea to make business process more efficient. A common buzzword of those days was *downsizing*. BPR failed its goal; downsizing was associated with layoffs and more work for the employees and not with the ultimate efficiency goal. Reengineering proposed that the existing processes be discarded and new ones be created from scratch. This was a big and ambitious approach, a big bang change for the organization.

At the beginning of 2000, the term BPM was coined to refer to a new management approach, a holistic way to produce an agile and adaptive organization based on the enhancement of business processes. BPM unlike BPR is based in an incremental approach, improving the process step by step, with enough evidence to support this move. BPM is an old approach to manage processes, which has been renewed by using technology as the improvement tool.

With the advent of IT as a strategic partner and change enabler of the business, **Business Process Management Systems (BPMS)** appeared to support the BPM way of doing things.

Both BPR and BPM are based on the rational analysis of a business process from every possible dimension, destructuring it into its parts and relations, stripping the unproductive activities. BPR didn't take technology tools into account, but BPM advocates technology and feedback as the drivers of business process efficiency. BPM tries to automate as many activities as possible. Iterating as many times as needed, obtaining feedback, and making incremental changes to the process is the BPM mantra.

Efficiency is not the only goal of BPM. Companies are trying to gain a competitive edge over their competitors by perfecting their processes. A better process can win a customer; for example, in customer service a better process should reduce time to market and eliminate unnecessary internal bureaucracy.

Business Process Improvement

The first BPM process improvement efforts started a few years ago with the replacement of the BPR methodology, forcing companies to rethink their strategy in operational efficiency and placing processes in a strategic place.

The first effect was creating a **Business Process Improvement (BPI)** area in every process-led organization in order to take care of process design, enhancement, and monitoring. Technology is a key change enabler in BPI, so it's not uncommon to see IT departments very involved in BPI projects.

BPM efforts generally take more than an iteration to get the process right. So you must analyze the existing process, add the improvement, and then take feedback from the real-world operation. Then, you go back to the scratchboard, analyze the feedback (both numeric and from people), and add some other improvements until **Key Process Indicators (KPI)** are met. KPI are metrics that ensure that a process is running in its appropriate level of service, and are used to measure its **Service Level Agreements (SLA)**.

Business functions can agree a service level with other business functions within the same company or with business partners and customers. The goal of BPM is to make the process exceed or maintain its current SLA.

Every effort to change a business process must take people into the equation. People have a hard time adapting to new roles, functions, and procedures and can really subvert the effort of BPM. BPR considered people as numbers, replaceable material, and this was a key factor for its failure.

What's a BPMS?

Business Process Management Systems (BPMS) technology is a tool that implements BPM in the enterprise. BPMS suites are designed to model, execute, and optimize business-process models, helping BPM people and executive-level managers to take the necessary steps for process improvement.

In the BPMS world, modeling, executing, and optimizing a business process is a continuous cycle and is therefore represented by a circle. The following figure is called the BPM lifecycle. It depicts the sequence of steps followed during the implementation of BPM in a process.

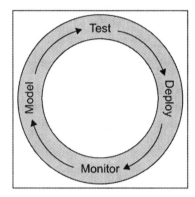

The BPM lifecycle begins by modeling the business process (taking an existing process or starting from scratch), followed by testing it, deploying it, and finally monitoring its execution in a production environment.

The first step is process modeling. It includes a phase of analysis if the modeling is being done for an existing process and if the modeling is being done for a new process, then it includes a design phase. Modeling is usually done by a business analyst who identifies and connects the basic building blocks of the process such as activities, roles, data, and so on. The next figure shows a business process modeling environment. It corresponds to OSDesigner, the business process modeler included in OSWorkflow.

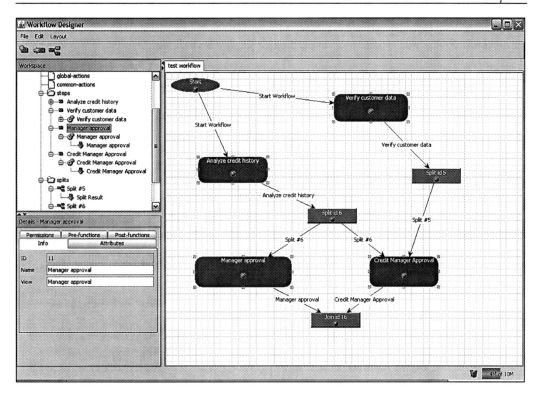

As shown in the figure, a process is being created visually, by specifying the steps and the transition among them.

The testing phase consists of two steps, namely, validation and verification. Validation asserts correctness of the solution while verification checks conformity to the requirements. These activities include several debug iterations and test runs in a development or testing environment.

Once the process model is known to be correct, the analyst or programmer deploys the model in a process engine. This engine parses and identifies the model, and then executes the instructions and actions associated with it. The next step is monitoring the process in place.

During monitoring, we spot the bottlenecks, superfluous steps, and possible automation activities. Monitoring the process is usually a visual activity, through the use of a **Business Activity Monitoring (BAM)** dashboard. The BAM dashboard, also known as the BAM console, is a visual aggregation of business process information, usually real-time information. The figure next page shows a typical BAM dashboard, which includes charts and gauges to display the different metrics of a business process.

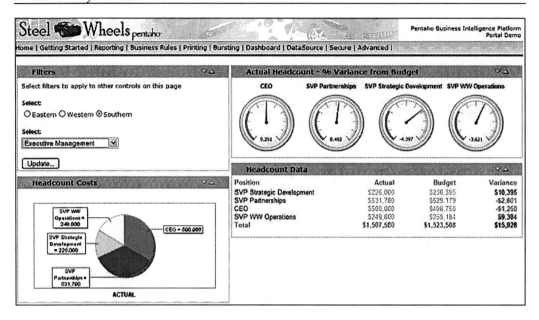

In the meantime, we must take care of unforeseen environmental changes, like laws and regulations that have an impact on the process and the company. Regulations usually demand businesses to have a very good visibility of their processes, as well as their inputs and outputs.

The optimization can be done manually from the feedback obtained in production or can be simulated from artificial or historical load. The optimization must be modeled again, restarting the BPM lifecycle. The BPM cycle can be repeated until the business process performs like a fine-tuned machine.

Traceability and Auditing

BPMS also adds traceability and auditing to a business process. When the BPMS workflow engine executes an activity it registers a trace or audit log. This log commonly includes context data, such as the current user, the process instance ID, an activity start and end timestamp, and other useful data.

Traceability supports two goals—operational and strategic. The operational goal helps users in searching for information about the process and exposes the current activity and state of the system. The strategic goal enables the users to know where the bottleneck of a process is, and where they must tune the process for maximum efficiency. The following screenshot shows sample traceability data from a business process.

AUDIT TRACE

STEP	START	FINISH	STATUS	USERNAME	ACTION
Start	07/09/2006 13:17	13/12/2006 15:51	In progress	JANE DOE	Finish
	07/09/2006 13:18			JOHN DOE	Acquire
	13/12/2006 15:50			JANE DOE	Release
	13/12/2006 15:50			JANE DOE	Acquire
Finish	13/12/2006 15:51		Finishing		Ninguna
Start	15/12/2006 17:07	15/12/2006 17:09	iniciado	GUEZIKARAIAN EDGA...	Finish

CLOSE   PRINT

The traceability data in the screenshot shows the transition from step to step, the user that caused the transition, the time, and the current status, as well as other context information.

Traceability data is a goldmine for Business Intelligence as it includes a lot of hidden patterns about usage and operation of the process.

Through the use of data-mining software, you can uncover these patterns to understand your business, customers, and suppliers in a better way.

Different Kinds of BPMS

Every business process has two types of tasks—manual and automated. Manual tasks require essential intervention of a human being, whereas automated tasks are done by computers or machines. A number of BPMS tools are suited to the human aspect, some support only the automated level, and others can implement end-to-end processes without hassle. These are commonly called people to people, system to system, and people to system BPMS.

System Orchestration with System-Oriented BPMS

First, we will talk about the system to system BPMS, so let's see how they were born in order to understand them well.

Some BPMS suites are descendants of **Enterprise Application Integration (EAI)** tools. EAI began in the mid-nineties to break the barriers placed in the way of integration of legacy systems. Legacy systems were separated into vertical silos and the integration of information and functionality was difficult, costly, and error prone.

Every application that needed to share or gain information from another system had to program a custom interface or connector for integration, thereby taking away time, money, and most importantly agility and flexibility to change.

EAI alleviated this problem by using proprietary connectors to legacy systems and having a central broker of information. This central broker had the ability to talk to several heterogeneous legacy systems (such as ERP, CRM, custom applications, and so on) and made the overall integration process much easier.

Integration became more affordable and faster, but the need for custom connectors made the solution expensive and provider dependent. These custom connectors used the proprietary language of the systems they were integrating, which made them expensive. There was no universal integration protocol to talk to every partner system.

The answer to a universal integration protocol came from standards like HTTP and XML. XML allows applications to share information without taking lower-level details such as the architecture of each system into account.

HTTP, originally designed for web navigation purposes, fit the bill of common transport. XML and HTTP, when used in combination to share information and functionality are called Web Services. The following figure shows an EAI broker sending and receiving information from different applications initially not suited to talk to each other.

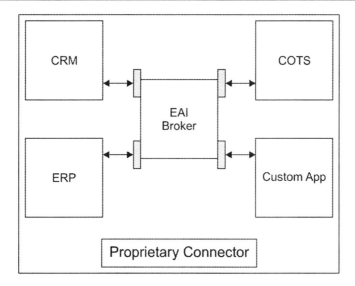

The use of Web Services technology by all applications to share information and functionality with each other has made the integration process much easier and standard based. This has brought down the integration costs and allowed companies to embrace business changes faster.

An architecture based on the integration of services is called a **Service-Oriented Architecture (SOA)**.

System Orchestration

Getting back to the different tasks of a business process, the automated activities are usually scattered across several systems, some core, some satellite, some legacy, and some new ones. The use of several disparate user interfaces and applications by an end user to perform a task such as an airline reservation is prone to error, lacks currency of the information, has a high training cost, and causes loses in productivity.

The main concept of system orchestration is to facilitate the business activity of the end user by eliminating the need for several separate information systems to realize the business process.

The orchestration systems query each system to gather information, combine this information, and feed it to other systems. So, to make an airline reservation, the airline clerk uses three to four systems. With orchestration this is reduced to a unique application. This scenario is very common in big companies where legacy systems are responsible for some tasks.

This has several benefits such as better information accuracy, reducing the information lag, and abstracting the end users from needing to know which systems have the functionality required. The following figure shows a sample orchestrator dynamic interaction between information systems.

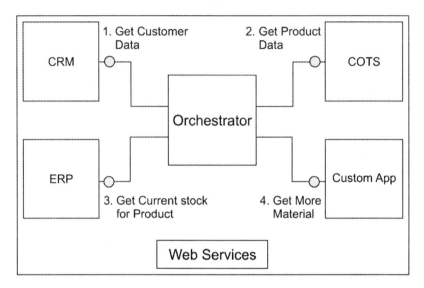

The orchestration enables us to have higher-level services and composite applications.

Higher-level services use existing infrastructure such as a service for giving customer details and another for customer credit details, and combine the information into one service.

Composite applications allow the user to use only one user interface to query several sources of information and services without knowing the rest of the applications.

Some BPM tools implement only the system orchestrator component and talk only the Web Services standard, while others also have custom connectors to share information with legacy systems.

System orchestration can be done with systems inside an enterprise or across industry partners or in companies using heterogeneous applications. The OSWorkflow workflow engine can be used as a system orchestrator to automate system interactions. We will talk about this in Chapter 7.

Enabling Workgroup Collaboration with People-Oriented BPMS

We have covered the automated part of a business process. Now, let's take a look at the manual tasks requiring frequent or mandatory human intervention.

In our day-to-day life, we often find ourselves coordinating activities with other coworkers. Business processes tend to require a lot of coordination and organization of people's work, and it grows exponentially with the number of people involved. It gets even more complex with a broad geographic distribution as is the case with multinational companies.

The successful completion of a business process depends on the coordination of the people.

BPMS technology can facilitate workgroup collaboration through sequencing of activities, reminders, alerts, escalations, automatic approvals, etc. This automates the operational and tedious task of coordination and enables collaboration between different company departments.

For human interaction, people-to-people BPMS suites provide a user interface (web, fat client, or email) for the users to interact with the business processes and collaborate with each other. Collaboration is sharing knowledge about a process or a work item, increasing productivity, and increasing communication between coworkers.

This user interface guides the user through the process, manages the user roles and to-do tasks, gives search capabilities, and other useful features.

The usability of this user interface is a critical success factor in the implementation of a human-oriented BPMS. The following figure shows a sample BPMS user interface suited for human interaction.

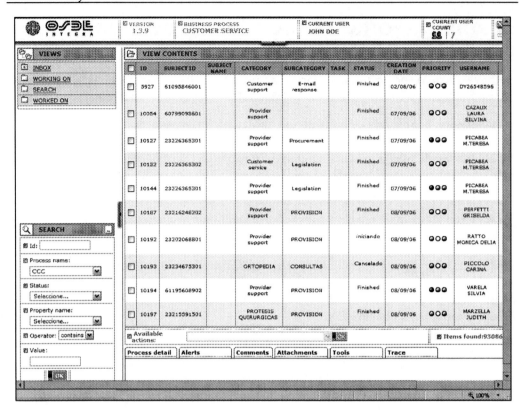

An important thing to notice from the screenshot is the user-friendliness of the interface. This interface orders the processes into folders with user-defined criteria and serves as a unique front end for all business processes. This means that the user interacts with all the business processes through this GUI thereby making the experience more consistent. Moreover, it is easier to use and so significantly less user training is needed.

Components of a BPM Solution

After knowing the different types of BPMS, you'll wonder about the components that make up a BPMS. The main components of a full-fledged BPM solution are as follows:

- Process Modeler
- Workflow Engine
- Business Rule Engine
- Graphical User interface (for human-oriented BPMS)
- Integration connectors (for system-oriented BPMS)
- BAM and BI tools

The following figure shows the *layers* of the solution with the workflow engine and the business rule engine as the main components on which the others are based.

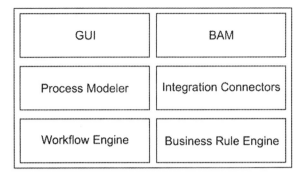

The Workflow Management Coalition

The **Workflow Management Coalition (WfMC)** is a non-profit organization constituted by users and vendors, dedicated to disseminating best practices about Workflow technology. The WfMC recommends the following model to architect workflow solutions:

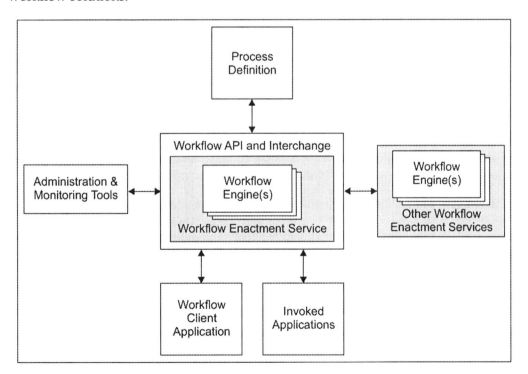

As shown in the figure, the WfMC specifies the Workflow Engine (as the Workflow Enactment Services and API), the Modeler (implicitly in the Process Definition), the BAM dashboard (as the Administration and Monitoring Tools), the GUI (in the client application block), and the integration connectors (via the Invoked Applications).

Let's examine each component in detail. The process modeler found in both human-oriented and system-oriented BPMS is usually a visual application that can be used by a business analyst and optionally by an end user. The modeler allows the user to define the process and describe the activities, decisions, rules, and so on.

The output generated by the modeler is a process definition that is executable by the workflow engine. The process definition is the set of activities, decisions, roles, etc. and the relationships between them.

The workflow engine is the core component of a BPM solution. It's in charge of initiating, maintaining state, and transitioning the business process, while managing security and roles.

The workflow engine takes the process definition as an input, executes it, and while the process is alive, it stores the process data into a traceability and auditing log. Additionally, it provides both synchronous and asynchronous execution of tasks. These tasks can be internal tasks such as state transition and external tasks such as integration connector invocations.

The workflow engine acts as a system orchestrator in system-oriented BPMS.

Rules for business processes are another facet of BPM solutions. Most companies have complex business rules in every process scattered through several legacy systems and these rules change frequently due to internal and external factors.

Efforts must be made to permit these rules to change rapidly, and be modified by anyone without technical skills, such as an end user. Externalization, definition, administration, and traceability of these rules are common features of rules engines.

The workflow engine calls business rules from inside the business process. Sometimes the business rules are embedded in the process definition and sometimes they are placed in an external application. There's a third scenario when the rules reside inside the business rule engine; this is the best place to foster reusability and uniqueness of the business rules.

For human-oriented BPMS, the critical component is the GUI. The GUI is the view of the business process allowing the users to interact with other components. Usability of this GUI is critical to the success of a BPM solution implementation.

On the other hand, integration connectors are a standard feature for system orchestration and EAI-oriented BPMS. These connectors handle the connection, mapping, chatting, validation, and error checking of interfaces to new and legacy systems. It's common to see an integration engine managing the connection pipeline, the input of a system is the output of a previous system, with its data mapped and transformed.

For the BPM circle to be fulfilled, users need to monitor the process, analyze it, and get feedback for improvement. BAM and BI tools enable real-time monitoring, alert activation, reporting, and statistics collection for the process.

BI allows the BPMS to exploit historical and real-time data; some suites even give forecasts from historical data. The BI component analyzes the traceability and auditing database to discover bottlenecks, gather statistics, and optimize the process.

For more information about the WfMC visit `http://www.wfmc.org/`.

How Components Map to the BPM Lifecycle

In the first section of the chapter, we saw the BPM lifecycle—the usual methodology to implement BPM in a single process or whole enterprise. The BPMS components align with this methodology by giving a tool for each part of the cycle. The next figure shows the mapping between components and the BPM lifecycle.

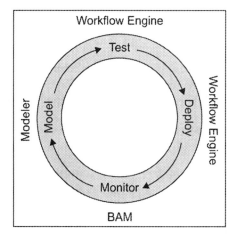

The modeling phase has the process modeler, the test and deployment (execution) phases uses the workflow engine, and finally the monitoring (optimization) phase is supported by the BAM.

Open-Source BPMS

This book discusses creating a complete open-source BPM solution stack using OSWorkflow, Pentaho, Quartz, JBoss Rules, and Esper, which are mature open-source solutions built with 100% Java code. The following figure shows the layers of our solution using open-source products.

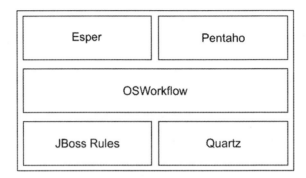

OSWorkflow covers the process modeler and workflow engine complemented by Quartz to make asynchronous tasks possible. JBoss Rules is the rule engine used to easily define and centralize rules. Pentaho and Esper make up the BAM. Pentaho deals with the reporting and analysis and Esper with active event notifications enabling proactive monitoring.

Summary

This chapter serves as an introduction to BPM technology, its goals and vision, exposing much of its history and terminologies. With this background, you can add value in architecting and developing enterprise BPMS or simple workflows.

In the next chapters we will cover in detail the open-source stack of products used to build completely free BPM solutions.

This book has been broken into eight chapters, with the first one introducing the BPM technology and its context, chapters two to four covering the OSWorkflow concepts from basic to advanced uses, and chapters five to eight showing how to integrate different open-source products to enhance the OSWorkflow functionality. These products are JBoss Rules, OpenSymphony's Quartz, Codehaus's Esper, and finally the Pentaho reporting engine.

Each chapter will present a part of the BPMS solution.

2

OSWorkflow Introduction and Basics

This chapter introduces OSWorkflow and teaches the basics of the workflow engine. We begin by describing a simple real-world example, and then by using steps, actions, and results we create an XML definition of the process. We have taken the example of the holiday workflow, which is used in every company.

After building the example, we will show you how to visually model workflow definitions. Finally, we will embed OSWorkflow into our application or use it as a standalone workflow engine. The outline will cover the following topics:

- Downloading and installing OSWorkflow
- Getting a taste from the distribution
- OSWorkflow basics
- Visual Process modeling
- Ways to implement OSWorkflow

Downloading and Installing OSWorkflow

The current OSWorkflow version, 2.8, requires a Java VM version 1.3 or higher. You can download binaries and sources from the OSWorkflow page at `http://www.opensymphony.com/osworkflow/`. To use the software, you must unpack the files using any compression utility like 7-Zip.

In the binary version you already have everything you need to run, on the other hand, the source code distribution must be compiled using the Jakarta Ant utility.

Getting a Taste from the Distribution

The OSWorkflow distribution comes with a sample web application useful for testing workflow definitions. This test application is packed as a WAR file, called `osworkflow-2.8.0-example.war`. In order to deploy it, you will need to install a web container such as Jakarta Tomcat.

You can download Tomcat from `http://tomcat.apache.org`. After downloading, unpack the distribution to a directory, and copy the `osworkflow-2.8.0-example.war` file into the `webapps` directory inside the root directory of Tomcat.

After that, start Tomcat by executing the `startup.bat` file in the `bin` directory of the distribution (or `startup.sh` if you are in a UNIX system). When Tomcat starts, open your web browser and point it to the following address: `http://localhost:8080/osworkflow-2.8.0-example.war` (change the host and port to the one on which you configured Tomcat; the default is localhost listening on port 8080). We are going to navigate through the generic user interface supplied with OSWorkflow.

The WAR distribution is configured by default with a sample publishing workflow definition and the workflow's persistence is done in the system's memory, so you can try it out.

Navigating the Sample User Interface

OSWorkflow includes a sample workflow definition based in a document-publishing system. Be free to try it out; log into the web application and execute actions. The screenshots that follow will show you how to instantiate a new document publishing workflow, revise the history and traceability data, and search for workflows in the workflow database.

The welcome screen that appears immediately after you enter the application address into the browser is as follows:

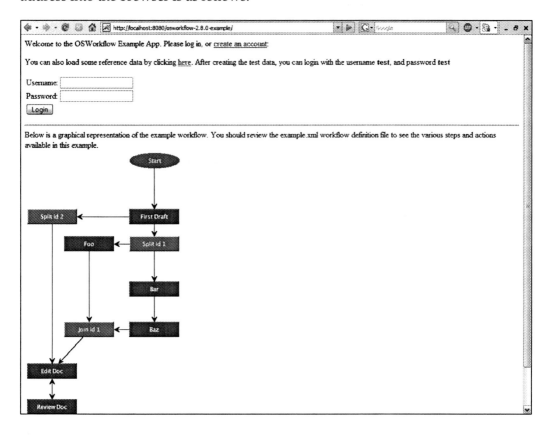

It shows a login screen with two hyperlinks—one for loading test users and the other for creating a new account.

Click the reference data hyperlink to load the test user's data. After loading the data, you can log in using "test" as username and password. Clicking the **Login** button will display the following screen:

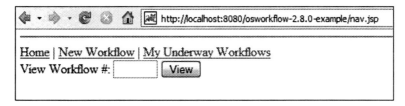

Once you are logged in, you will see the following three buttons:

- **Home**: This sends you back to the previous screen.
- **New Workflow**: This instantiates a new document-publishing workflow.
- **My Underway Workflows**: This shows you a list of workflows with the status "**Underway**". The significance of this status will be explained later in this chapter.

You will also see a **View Workflow** text box and a **View** button. Every time you create a new workflow, it is assigned a new identifier. Typing this identifier in the **View Workflow** text box and clicking the **View** button will show the workflow's traceability data. As we haven't generated any new workflows so far, we will cover this functionality later.

Clicking on **New Workflow** creates a new workflow instance, and stores it in memory, so don't be afraid to try it. After that click the anchor (**#**), to view the following page:

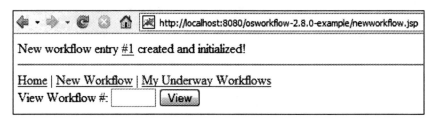

This window is the same as the one shown earlier with the only difference being the message **New workflow entry #1 created and initialized!** This message gives us the identifier number of the newly generated workflow. Clicking **#1** will show the workflow instance details and history steps as shown in the following screenshot:

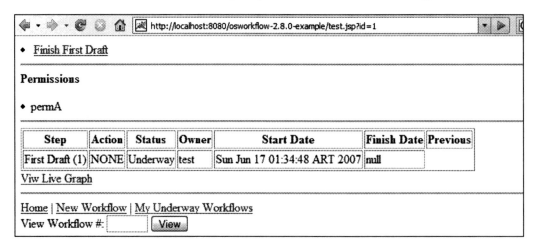

This window contains some very useful information, so let's look at it in detail.

The **Finish First Draft** hyperlink is the action used to execute the current step of the workflow. Below this hyperlink is a bulleted list, which enumerates the permissions needed for executing the **Finish First Draft** action. Under the **Permissions** section, resides the most important part of the application—the workflow's history and traceability data. At the moment, it is only showing where this workflow instance stands in the process flow.

The table shown in the figure consists of the following columns:

- **Step**: This column shows the history or the current step name.
- **Action**: This column displays the action executed to make the transition to this step. In this example the **Action** is **NONE**, which indicates that this is the first step.
- **Status**: This column gives the step status. In this example it is **Underway**. This status should not be confused with the process status. These concepts will be explained in detail later in the chapter.
- **Start Date**: This column tells the reader when the step started. The **Start Date** for this step is shown in the figure.
- **Finish Date**: This column tells the reader when the step ended. At the moment, we don't have a **Finish Date** because we haven't made the transition to another step as yet.
- **Previous**: This column tells us that no preceding steps were transited on the way to this step, as this is the first step in the workflow.

The **View Live Graph** hyperlink shows a graphical representation of the workflow descriptor.

Below this hyperlink are the same **Home**, **New Workflow**, and **My Underway Workflows** links for navigating away from this page.

The graph generated by **View Live Graph** is as follows:

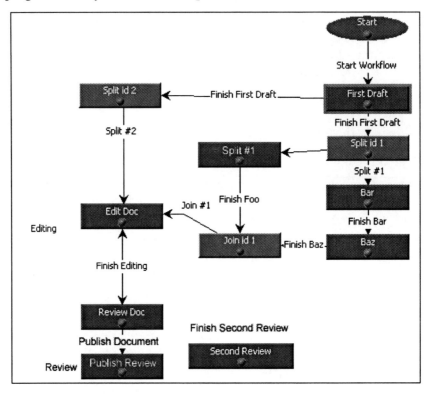

The red highlighted box is the current step of the workflow instance while the blue ones show steps and the gray ones are the splits and joins. Clicking **Finish First Draft** executes this action on the workflow #1 and puts the workflow in another step. The application will display the following screenshot, which is almost the same as the previous one. Let's take a look at the changes.

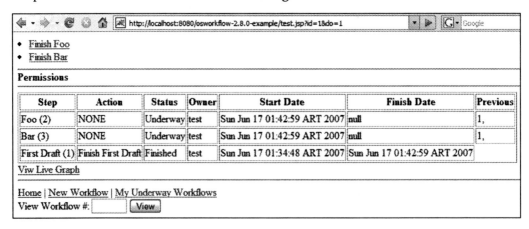

The first things you will notice are the **Finish Foo** and **Finish Bar** actions. These are two dummy actions in the document-publishing process. Below these actions is the **Permissions** section, which shows that the application doesn't need any permission for executing these actions. The history and traceability data table reflects a few changes—two more lines have been added to the table: Both are current steps in the workflow (because the **Finish First Draft** action caused the flow to split into two parallel branches). The **Status** of both is **Underway** and the **Previous** column shows **1**, indicating that both steps come from the first step. The step that previously was current is now a history step. It now has a **Finish Date** and the **Status** is **Finished**.

Try clicking the next actions to complete the document-publishing process. Eventually, you will finish some processes and they will not come back again in the **My Underway Workflows** page.

You can explore the interface a little bit, though it is very limited. The main purpose for which you can use this web application is for testing the process with your users thus skipping the prototype step. So let's learn the OSWorkflow constructs to deploy our chapter's example, the employee holidays business process.

OSWorkflow Basics

OSWorkflow is a mature open-source Java workflow engine. It is mainly aimed at the programmer and not an end user or business analyst. For the end user or business analyst, it includes a user-friendly visual workflow modeler designed only for basic usage.

This section will cover the basic concepts needed to create simple but useful process definitions using OSWorkflow. In the next section, we will generate a simple workflow to request holidays and finally you will have a complete working process. The example includes creating a very simple definition and the instantiation of new processes based on that descriptor.

XML Definition Files

OSWorkflow defines the process definition in an XML file called workflow descriptor. The OSWorkflow descriptor XML must have a root element of `workflow` and obligatory child elements named `steps` and `initial-actions`. Here is a snippet of the sample file bundled with the distribution.

```
<?xml version="1.0" encoding="UTF-8"?>
<!DOCTYPE workflow PUBLIC "-//OpenSymphony Group//DTD OSWorkflow
  2.6//EN" "http://www.opensymphony.com/osworkflow/workflow_2_8.dtd">
<workflow>
...
</workflow>
```

The workflow engine parses this file and builds the business process structure from the definition. You can construct any workflow definition by placing XML elements that represent workflow concepts such as steps and actions.

The XML file has a **Document Type Definition (DTD)** for validation purposes included with the OSWorkflow distribution. This allows any XML editor (such as Cooktop http://www.xmlcooktop.com/) to build syntactically correct definitions. The following figure depicts the OSWorkflow concept model.

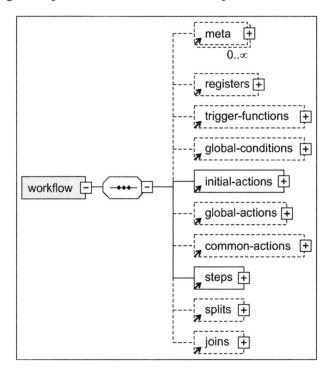

In the next section, we will explore the different constructs OSWorkflow has to assemble in a definition.

An Example Workflow

We will use a business process that a medium to large company would encounter at least once a year—the holiday workflow. Every time you need days to rest or travel, you request your supervisor to sanction the holidays. The supervisor may allow or deny the holidays.

The following flowchart shows the business process structure:

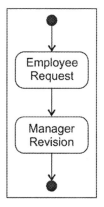

This is the simplest business process to start exploring the OSWorkflow features.

Steps, Actions, and Results: The Workflow Building Blocks

OSWorkflow's description of a business process is based on the concept of a *step*. A process has well-defined steps or activities to fulfill the business goal. For instance, the holiday workflow may have at least two logical steps—the employee's request and the manager's authorization.

Remember that every business process starts with external stimuli; in OSWorkflow these stimuli are called `initial-actions`. The `initial-actions` allow the workflow to start in a step other than the first, giving a lot of flexibility to the definition. The `initial-actions` element contains a group of `action` elements identified by numbers. You can explicitly start a workflow instance triggering a specific action. These actions can change the flow of control by going to different steps depending on a conditional element. We will discuss the `Conditional` constructs of OSWorkflow in the next chapter.

The following XML workflow definition snippet shows the typical beginning of a process definition:

```
<?xml version="1.0" encoding="UTF-8"?>
<!DOCTYPE workflow PUBLIC "-//OpenSymphony Group//
                                DTD OSWorkflow 2.6//EN"
                          "http://www.opensymphony.com/
                          osworkflow/workflow_2_8.dtd">
<workflow>
```

```
<initial-actions>
 <action id="100" name="Start Workflow">
  <results>
   <unconditional-result old-status="Finished" status="Underway"
                                                  step="1"/>
  </results>
 </action>
</initial-actions>
 ...
```

The definition starts with a DTD declaration that every valid XML document has and the root XML element, `workflow`. The DTD allows XML parsers and editors to validate every XML element and attribute thus generating a valid definition.

Every well-defined XML document starts and ends with only one root element. This `initial-action` construct indicates that the workflow will start immediately in step 1. The step is the main workflow concept in OSWorkflow because the process steps mark its progress and completion level. The next fragment follows the `initial-actions` element:

```
 ...
 <steps>
  <step id="1" name="Employee request">
   <actions>
   <action id="1" name="Request holidays">
    <results>
    <unconditional-result old-status="Finished" step="2"
                                              status="Requested"/>
    </results>
    </action>
   </actions>
  </step>
 ...
```

The `steps` XML element contains sibling `step` elements. In this snippet only one `step` element is present. In the definition snippet, we can see that `step` 1 is called `Employee request`.

Every step can have one or more actions, which can be viewed as events or external stimuli to the process that can occur in real life. In the manager authorization step, the manager can approve or deny the holidays. The definition says that `step 1` — the employee request phase — has only one `action` called `Request holidays` having ID 1. Actions must have a numerical ID that is unique within the definition.

Every action has at least one outcome, that is, a transition to the same or another step. The outcomes are called results, and the default outcome is the `unconditional-result` of an action. An `action` must have at least one default outcome; the other optional outcomes are called conditional results. The `Request holidays` action has an `unconditional-result` that brings the workflow to step 2.

```
...
<unconditional-result old-status="Finished" step="2"
                                            status="Requested"/>
...
```

You must be curious about the `old-status` and `status` attributes of the `unconditional-result` element. We'll cover both these attributes later in this chapter.

Conditional results have nested `conditions` elements, which are evaluated when going out of the step. The conditional results are executed only if the condition becomes true. Nested `conditions` can be combined with Boolean logic, such as AND and OR. If you have more than one conditional result in an `action`, the first one evaluated to true is followed.

Results can transition into a step, a join, or a split. The last two concepts will be covered later in the section.

Coming back to the example workflow, the manager can approve or deny (two independent actions) the request. The `finish` attribute set to TRUE signals OSWorkflow to finish the workflow after executing the action.

```
<step id="2" name="Manager revision">
 <actions>
  <action id="2" name="Approve" finish="TRUE">
   <results>
   <unconditional-result old-status="Revised" status="Approved" />
   </results>
  </action>
  <action id="3" name="Deny" finish="TRUE">
   <results>
   <unconditional-result old-status="Revised" status="Denied" />
   </results>
  </action>
 </actions>
</step>
```

You can imagine the `step` as a place, the `action` as an event, and the `result` as an exit path. So a workflow is composed of a series of `steps`. The `conditional results` are exits with doors that open if the associated predicate is true; the `unconditional result` is the path you'd take if all other exits are closed.

Optionally, if the manager approves or denies the request, we can send an email to the employee. A utility Java function included with the OSWorkflow distribution can take care of sending the email as you can see in the following fragment:

```
...
<action id="3" name="Deny" finish="TRUE">
    <pre-functions>
        <function type="class">
 <arg name="class.name">com.opensymphony.workflow.util.SendEmail
                                                        </arg>
            <arg name="to">dnlazo@osde.com.ar</arg>
            <arg name="from">dnlazo@osde.com.ar</arg>
            <arg name="subject">Holidays</arg>
            <arg name="cc">dnlazo@osde.com.ar</arg>
            <arg name="message">Your request has been denied</arg>
            <arg name="smtpHost">10.250.0.168</arg>
        </function>
    </pre-functions>
    <results>
        ...
    </results>
</action>
...
```

Stitching the fragments together, the definition ended up like this:

```
<?xml version="1.0" encoding="UTF-8"?>
<!DOCTYPE workflow PUBLIC "-//OpenSymphony Group//
                                    DTD OSWorkflow 2.8//EN"
                            "http://www.opensymphony.com/
                            osworkflow/workflow_2_8.dtd">
<workflow>
    <initial-actions>
        <action id="100" name="Start Workflow">
            <results>
                <unconditional-result old-status=
                            "Finished" status="Underway" step="1" />
            </results>
        </action>
    </initial-actions>

    <steps>
        <step id="1" name="Employee request">
            <actions>
                <action id="1" name="Request holidays">
```

```
            <results>
               <unconditional-result old-status=
                        "Finished" step="2" status="Requested" />
            </results>
         </action>
      </actions>
   </step>

   <step id="2" name="Manager revision">
      <actions>
         <action id="2" name="Approve" finish="TRUE">
            <results>
               <unconditional-result old-status=
                           "Revised" status="Approved" />
            </results>
         </action>

         <action id="3" name="Deny" finish="TRUE">
            <results>
               <unconditional-result old-status=
                              "Revised" status="Denied" />
            </results>
         </action>
      </actions>
   </step>
</steps>
</workflow>
```

This XML shows a workflow definition with two steps, the first with only one action, and the second with two actions, either one finishing the process. This example is very basic and linear; it proceeds in sequence. You can find the definition in the holiday.xml file. This file is included in the downloadable source code.

Testing the Workflow Definition

We can use the sample web application as a user-friendly way to test our definitions. We'll run our first definition this way. First, we must change to the webapps directory of the Tomcat distribution, unpack the osworkflow-2.8.0-example. war inside the webapps directory, and then delete the original WAR file. This way the example application will be deployed on what's called an expanded WAR, a directory resembling a WAR file. This allows us to tinker with the files without the hassle of repacking to a WAR file every time we change a file.

Then go inside the `osworkflow-2.8.0-example.war` folder, browse to the `WEB-INF/classes` folder, and rename the `example.xml` file to `example.xml.orig`. Then place the `holiday.xml` file included with the book and rename it to `example.xml`. This will cheat the sample web application into using our definition instead of the original publishing workflow definition.

That's it, now start up Tomcat again and point your web browser to `http://localhost:8080/osworkflow-2.8.0-example`, login, and enjoy your first business process. You can test every definition we will create in the book this way, or you can use the text-based test interface inside the `packtpub.osw.TestWorkflow` class. You can find all the directions inside the class javadoc comments.

Splits and Joins

In real-world situations, you can find employees collaborating and working simultaneously in parallel, in which case the process splits into two or more branches, and these branches can eventually join into a main path.

OSWorkflow has the split and join constructs to represent this situation. The split construct branches the main flow of the workflow into two parallel paths and the join construct does the opposite, it unites the branches into the main flow again.

Let's modify the chapter's example a little bit by saying that two managers must approve or deny the request. The first manager is the line or functional manager and the other is the human resources manager. Both managers must give their approval for the employee to receive an email confirming the approved status of his or her request. The following figure depicts the new business process:

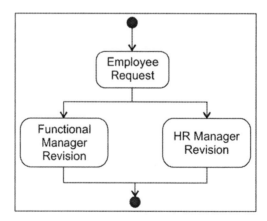

We will modify the XML definition to reflect this change by incorporating a `splits` and a `joins` XML element. The code snippet that follows shows the modification to the holiday example XML. The `splits` and the `joins` elements are children of the root `workflow` element.

```xml
<workflow>
...
<splits>
   <split id="1">
      <unconditional-result old-status="Finished" status="Underway"
step="2" />
      <unconditional-result old-status="Finished" status="Underway"
step="3" />
   </split>
</splits>

<joins>
   <join id="1">
      <conditions type="AND">
         <condition type="beanshell">
            <arg name="script">
               <![CDATA[
                     propertySet.setString("result", "denied");
                     if(jn.getStep(2).getStatus().endsWith("approved")
                     &&
                     jn.getStep(3).getStatus().endsWith("approved")){
                        propertySet.setString("result", "approved");
                     }
               </arg>
            </condition>
      </conditions>

      <unconditional-result old-status=
                        "JoinFinished" status="${result}" step="4" />
   </join>
</joins>
...
</workflow>
```

The `splits` element nests child `split` elements, each one telling the engine to fork the current path of execution into two parallel branches. The `split` must have an `id` and two results (one can be conditional but at least one must be unconditional). Each result's `step` attribute indicates to OSWorkflow to make this step the new current step. In this case, we have only one split identified by the number 1 and it will fork the process flow into two branches; the first one will go to step 2 and the other to step 3.

To arrive to a split, the conditional or unconditional result of a step must have the split attribute with the corresponding split ID as shown in the following snippet:

```
<step id="1" name="Step 1">
    <actions>
        <action id="1" name="Action 1">
            <results>
                <unconditional-result old-status="Finished"
status="Pending" split="1"/>
            </results>
        </action>
    </actions>
</step>
```

This fragment tells OSWorkflow that the unconditional result of Step 1 is to go to split 1. Similarly to the splits element, the joins element can have any number of join child elements you want. Each join has at least one condition. To be able to use a join node, the process must have executed a split previously.

When the engine arrives at a join, it evaluates all the conditions. If they all return true, then the unconditional result is followed. A join has a join condition and a new jn variable. This new variable is available only on join conditions and has several convenient methods to check for workflow and step status. Let's analyze the joins section in more detail:

```
<joins>
    <join id="1">
        <conditions type="AND">
            <condition type="beanshell">
                <arg name="script">
                    <![CDATA[
                        propertySet.setString("result", "denied");
                        if(jn.getStep(2).getStatus().endsWith("approved")
                        &&
                        jn.getStep(3).getStatus().endsWith("approved")){
                            propertySet.setString("result", "approved");
                        }
                </arg>
            </condition>
        </conditions>

        <unconditional-result old-status=
                        "JoinFinished" status="${result}" step="4" />
    </join>
</joins>
```

Here we have only one join identified by the number 1. To effectively join two parallel branches of execution, the process will have to comply with a condition scripted in BeanShell code. We will cover BeanShell functions and conditions in Chapter 4; for now assume that the code will check for the status of step 2 and step 3 to be approved. If any of them is not approved, the process will stay in whatever step it currently is in. When the condition is satisfied, the flow of control will be directed to the fourth step (see the `unconditional-result` element).

One last important thing to note: A split or a join cannot result into a split or join again; this is a current limitation of OSWorkflow.

Setting Status and Old Status Values

A workflow always has a state associated with it; OSWorkflow represents it in the form of status. Every step has a status while the workflow is placed on it and when the workflow advances, OSWorkflow assigns the leaving step an `old-status` value. Consider the previous example:

```
<step id="2" name="Manager revision">
    <actions>
        <action id="2" name="A+pprove">
            <results>
                <unconditional-result old-status=
                            "Revised" status="Approved" step="3"/>
            </results>
        </action>
```

When the action with `id` 2 makes the process take the action's unconditional result, it leaves the step with the status `Revised` (thus an old status) and the new current step (step 3) takes the status value of `Approved`. The following figure shows this mechanism in a more generic fashion. It depicts a step transition from `Step 1` to `Step 2`.

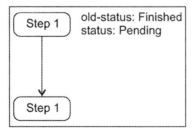

The definition of Step 1 is as follows:

```
<step id="1" name="Step 1">
    <actions>
        <action id="1" name="Action 1">
            <results>
                <unconditional-result old-status=
                            "Finished" status="Pending" step="2"/>
            </results>
        </action>
    </actions>
</step>
```

As Step 1 transitions to Step 2 it set its old-status value to Finished and Step 2 status to Pending.

The status and old-status values are nominal; you can define them to whatever value you want. The most common status names are "Pending" or "Queued". And the old-status is typically "Finished".

A common question an end user has on workflows is — what is the current state of this process? As OSWorkflow supports parallel steps, the answer is — the status of every current step.

As the workflow advances, the engine calls the completed steps "history steps" and the current steps are called well, just "current steps". When a workflow is finished, it has steps only in history and none in the current stage.

Sending an Email Automatically

In the new example workflow definition, if both managers approve the request, then OSWorkflow sends a mail message notifying about this. If one of the managers denies the request, another mail message is sent. You can see in the following snippet the pre-functions and function elements:

```
...
<step id="4" name="Notify employee">
    <actions>
        <action id="6" name="Notify" finish="TRUE">
            <pre-functions>
                <function type="class">
                    <arg name="class.name">com.opensymphony.workflow.util.
SendEmail</arg>
                    <arg name="to">to@osworkflow.com.ar</arg>
                    <arg name="from">from@osworkflow.com.ar</arg>
                    <arg name="subject">Holidays</arg>
```

```
            <arg name="cc">cc@osworkflow.com.ar</arg>
            <arg name="message">Your request has been ${result}
                                                            </arg>
            <arg name="smtpHost">10.250.0.168</arg>
        </function>
    </pre-functions>
    <results>
        <unconditional-result old-status="Finished" status=
                                    "Line approval" step="-1" />
    </results>
  </action>
 </actions>
</step>
  ...
```

This snippet sends an email with a destination address, a "from" mail address, and a carbon copy. This is intended to be sent to the employee; as the subject of the email is "Holidays" the content of the email varies. If the holiday request was approved it will say "Your request has been approved", if it was rejected it will say so. The ${result} token and more about the OSWorkflow functions will be explained later in the chapter.

Let's go back to actions; they can have functions, which are the main extensibility mechanism of OSWorkflow. They are of the following two kinds: pre-functions and post-functions. Additionally, OSWorkflow functions can be action based or step based. Action pre-functions execute before the execution of the action and Action post-functions execute during the transition. Functions and OSWorkflow's built-in functions will be seen in more depth in Chapter 4.

```
            <pre-functions>
                <function type="class">
                    <arg name="class.name">
                            com.opensymphony.workflow.util.SendEmail </arg>
                    <arg name="to">dnlazo@osde.com.ar</arg>
                    <arg name="from">dnlazo@osde.com.ar</arg>
                    <arg name="subject">Holidays</arg>
                    <arg name="cc">dnlazo@osde.com.ar</arg>
                    <arg name="message">
                                    Your request has been ${result}</arg>
                    <arg name="smtpHost">10.250.0.168</arg>
                </function>
            </pre-functions>
```

Pre-functions are executed before the step transitions to the next step.

Our modified holiday workflow definition ended up like this:

```xml
<?xml version="1.0" encoding="UTF-8"?>
<!DOCTYPE workflow PUBLIC "-//OpenSymphony Group//DTD OSWorkflow 2.6//
EN" "http://www.opensymphony.com/osworkflow/workflow_2_8.dtd">
<workflow>
   <initial-actions>
      <action id="100" name="Start Workflow">
         <results>
            <unconditional-result old-status=
                           "Finished" status="Underway" step="1" />
         </results>
      </action>
   </initial-actions>

   <steps>
      <step id="1" name="Employee request">
         <actions>
            <action id="1" name="Request holidays">
               <results>
                  <unconditional-result old-status=
                           "Finished" split="1" status="Requested" />
               </results>
            </action>
         </actions>
      </step>

      <step id="2" name="Line Manager revision">
         <actions>
            <action id="2" name="Approve">
               <results>
                  <unconditional-result old-status=
                           "Line aproved" status="joining" join="1" />
               </results>
            </action>

            <action id="3" name="Deny">
               <results>
                  <unconditional-result old-status=
                           "Line denied" status="joining" join="1" />
               </results>
            </action>
         </actions>
      </step>

      <step id="3" name="HR Manager revision">
```

```
        <actions>
            <action id="4" name="HR Approve">
                <results>
                    <unconditional-result old-status=
                              "HR aproved" status="joining" join="1" />
                </results>
            </action>

            <action id="5" name="HR Deny">
                <results>
                    <unconditional-result old-status=
                              "HR denied" status="joining" join="1" />
                </results>
            </action>
        </actions>
    </step>

    <step id="4" name="Notify employee">
        <actions>
            <action id="6" name="Notify" finish="TRUE">
                <pre-functions>
                    <function type="class">
                        <arg name="class.name">
                          com.opensymphony.workflow.util.SendEmail</arg>
                        <arg name="to">dnlazo@osde.com.ar</arg>
                        <arg name="from">dnlazo@osde.com.ar</arg>
                        <arg name="subject">Holidays</arg>
                        <arg name="cc">dnlazo@osde.com.ar</arg>
                        <arg name="message">
                                    Your request has been ${result}</arg>

                        <arg name="smtpHost">10.250.0.168</arg>
                    </function>
                </pre-functions>

                <results>
                    <unconditional-result old-status=
                         "Finished" status="Line approval" step="-1" />
                </results>
            </action>
        </actions>
    </step>
</steps>

<splits>
```

```
        <split id="1">
           <unconditional-result old-status=
                            "Finished" status="Underway" step="2" />

           <unconditional-result old-status=
                            "Finished" status="Underway" step="3" />
        </split>
     </splits>

     <joins>
        <join id="1">
           <conditions type="AND">
              <condition type="beanshell">
                 <arg name="script">
                    <![CDATA[
                          propertySet.setString("result", "denied");
                          if(jn.getStep(2).getStatus().
endsWith("aproved") && jn.getStep(3).getStatus().endsWith("aproved")){
                          propertySet.setString("result", "aproved");
                          }
                          !("Underway".equals(jn.getStep(2).
getStatus())) && !("Underway".equals(jn.getStep(3).getStatus()))
]]>
                 </arg>
              </condition>
           </conditions>

           <unconditional-result old-status=
                            "JoinFinished" status="${result}" step="4" />
        </join>
     </joins>
  </workflow>
```

This definition is a little more advanced than the first one. For starters it has a parallel path of execution, so two managers must approve the request independently. It also sends an email to the employee telling him or her the result of his or her request. This file is called holiday2.xml. In the next chapter, we will learn how to visually model workflow definitions using the built-in graphical tool of OSWorkflow.

Visual Process Modeling

Instead of writing the XML definition by hand, you can use the visual modeler. Although it's a little more restricted than the manual approach, it is very useful for non-technical people to specify a business process.

Visually Creating the Holiday Example

You can start the designer by typing `java -jar designer.jar` on the command line of your system (given that the `java` command is on your path). First copy `designer.jar` into the `lib/designer` path of your unpacked OSWorkflow distribution. You have to do this because some library files cannot be found otherwise hopefully this will be fixed in the next version of OSWorkflow.

After the splash screen, a blank workspace screen will be displayed, like the one that follows:

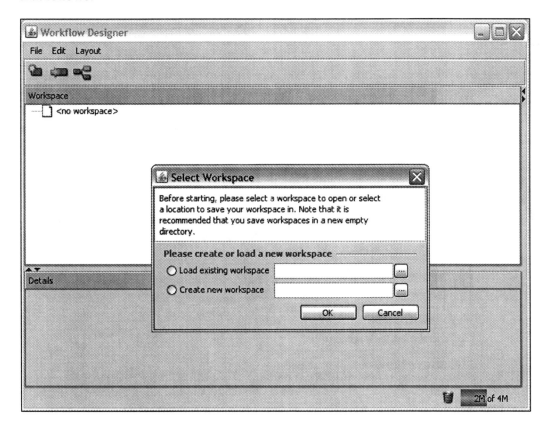

This welcome screen prompts you to load an existing workspace or create a new one. We will create a new workspace to model the same holiday example, but this time visually. In the **Select Workspace** dialog, select the **Create new workspace** checkbox, and click on the **...** button.

After clicking the button, a standard file chooser dialog will appear. You must navigate to a directory of your choice and type in a new filename for the workspace.

After creating a new workspace file, we continue by creating a new workflow. Go to the **File | New | New workflow** menu item and click on the item.

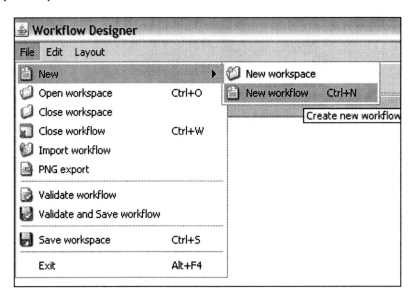

You will be prompted with a dialog box to type a name for the new workflow:

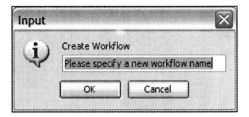

Type any name you want and, after clicking **OK**, a new workflow screen will appear as shown in the following figure. The three icons in the leftmost upper section of the screen are used to create a new step, split, or join. These are the building blocks of the definition.

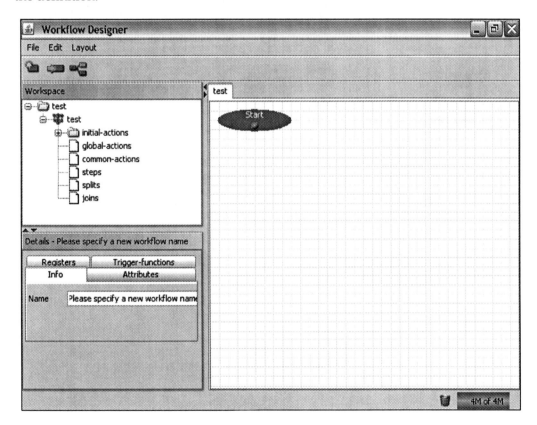

We will create a new step by clicking on the new step icon and then clicking on the empty canvas. A dialog box appears as shown in the following figure. This dialog box prompts us to select the result type of the transition between the start node and the new step. In this case, we will select **Unconditional**.

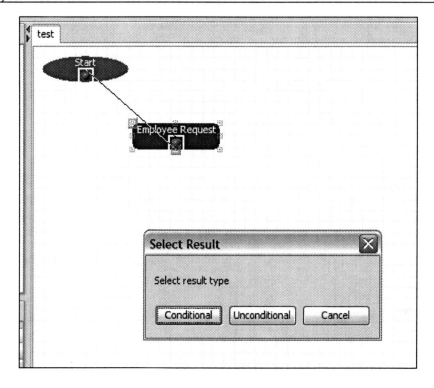

After we click the **Unconditional** button, the visual modeler will create a graphical link between the start and the **Employee Request** step. Then we proceed to make another step, called **Manager Revision**, again with the result type as unconditional.

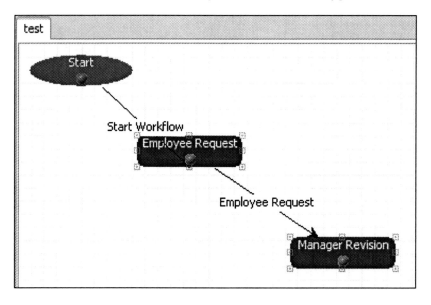

With this last step, we have finished the first and simplest holiday process definition. Go to **File | Save Workflow** to save the displayed contents in an XML file.

Looking at the End Result

Opening the definition in Notepad will display the following XML:

```
<?xml version="1.0" encoding="UTF-8"?>
<!DOCTYPE workflow PUBLIC "-//OpenSymphony Group//DTD OSWorkflow 2.8//
EN" "http://www.opensymphony.com/osworkflow/workflow_2_8.dtd">
<workflow>
  <meta name="lastModified">Sun Dec 17 16:57:01 ART 2006</meta>
  <meta name="created">Sun Dec 17 16:55:59 ART 2006</meta>
  <meta name="generator">OSWOrkflow Designer</meta>
  <initial-actions>
    <action id="0" name="Start Workflow">
      <results>
        <unconditional-result id="2" old-status=
                              "Finished" status="Queued" step="1"/>
      </results>
    </action>
  </initial-actions>
  <steps>
    <step id="1" name="Employee Request">
      <actions>
        <action id="4" name="Employee Request" view=
                                            "Employee Request">
          <results>
            <unconditional-result id="5" old-status=
                              "Finished" status="Queued" step="3"/>
          </results>
        </action>
      </actions>
    </step>
    <step id="3" name="Manager Authorization">
    </step>
  </steps>
</workflow>
```

Notice that the definition is not the same as the one made manually. This is because the visual modeler is suited for simpler business processes. The recommended approach for complex workflows is to build the definition manually.

Ways to Implement OSWorkflow

There are two ways of implementing OSWorkflow: the first is embedding OSWorkflow in your application and the second is using OSWorkflow as a standalone workflow server.

OSWorkflow as a Workflow Layer

If your needs are just workflow support in one application, then incorporating the OSWorkflow libraries and using the API is sufficient. An example application architecture diagram showing the **Business Process Layer** that is responsible for tracking the business process in the application is as follows:

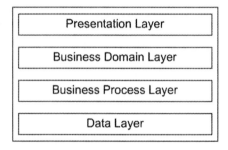

The addition of this layer to the standard three adds workflow capabilities to the domain model. This domain model contains the abstract entities of the business domain that travel with the business process. Remember, that each layer can talk only to the layers above and below, so the **Business Domain Layer** handles **Business Process Layer** objects. The section entitled *Embedding OSWorkflow into your Applications* in Chapter 4 will cover this architectural option.

OSWorkflow as a Centralized Workflow Server

If you need a corporate centralized workflow server, then you can execute OSWorkflow with SOAP bindings to have workflow functionality across applications. As long as you use SOAP as the transport protocol, you can integrate applications written in any programming language such as .NET, COBOL, and obviously Java.

The following figure depicts the role of the centralized workflow server:

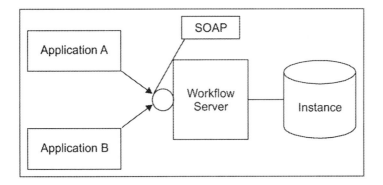

In the standalone environment, you have the advantage of centralizing business process data for the corporation and reusing workflow logic in applications. Having this information allows you to mine and explore the information to uncover hidden process patterns and process relationships. To enable other applications to use workflow server, it must have a universal connector, a SOAP web service interface.

Adding the SOAP Bindings

OSWorkflow uses the Codehaus XFire (http://xfire.codehaus.org/) library to expose a set of interfaces through the web services SOAP protocol. To enable the OSWorkflow's SOAP server, you have to use a web container such as Jakarta Tomcat. Create a web application, and then modify the application's web.xml descriptor present inside the application's WEB-INF directory to include the following lines:

```
<servlet>
    <servlet-name>SOAPWorkflow</servlet-name>
    <servlet-class>com.opensymphony.workflow.soap.SOAPWorkflowServlet
                                                    </servlet-class>
</servlet>

<servlet-mapping>
    <servlet-name>SOAPWorkflow</servlet-name>
    <url-pattern>/wsserver/*</url-pattern>
</servlet-mapping>
```

After modifying the `web.xml` file, put the XFire libraries (listed in the following table) inside the `WEB-INF/lib` directory of the web application.

Jar File	Description
jaxen-1.1-beta-5.jar	XPath expression parser
jdom-1.0.jar	DOM navigator library
stax-1.1.2-dev.jar	XML parser
wsdl4j-1.4.jar	WSDL library
xfire-aegis.jar	XFire support library
xfire-core.jar	XFire core library

Once the application is deployed, you can access the OSWorkflow's SOAP WSDL at `http://<server>/ wsserver/Workflow?wsdl`.

This WSDL is the web service descriptor and lists all the operations available in the web service. For the client applications you can use the XFire library or another SOAP client to access services of the OSWorkflow server. That's all you need to create a centralized workflow engine server for all your applications.

Summary

This chapter covered the most basics concepts to get you started with business process definitions using OSWorkflow as your workflow engine. The next chapter will cover advanced uses and will build upon the basic concepts.

3
Adding Code to our Definitions

This chapter introduces several key features of OSWorkflow like variable interpolation, OSWorkflow function providers, registers, conditions, and BeanShell scripting. These tools are useful for creating sophisticated business process definitions by adding custom code.

This chapter covers some advanced features available in OSWorkflow such as the ability to persist variables using `PropertySet`. We will learn how to check input data with our own validation rules using the OSWorkflow Validator model. Finally, we will cover two very handy definitions tips: `Auto` and `Finish` Actions, to make our definitions more compact.

How to Deal with Transient Data

Not every bit of data is created to be persisted; for these cases OSWorkflow provides a transient variables map. This map is created for every invocation to the `Workflow` instance and is used to store temporary data in one place during the workflow processing. Its content is cleared in each invocation and is pre-populated with the current workflow instance, store, and descriptor objects inside it. The input data from the outside is present in this map.

The transient variables map is made available for scripting to the `FunctionProviders` and `Condition` interfaces. In the BeanShell scripting context, the map variable is called `transientVars`.

For example, the following code snippet prints the content of a variable from the transient variable map:

```
<function type="beanshell">
  <arg name="script">
  System.out.println(transientVars.get("foo"))
  </arg>
</function>
```

Also, the following special variables are available in the `transientVars` map:

Map Key	Object class	Description
Entry	WorkflowEntry	The workflow instance.
Context	WorkflowContext	The workflow context.
actionId	Integer	ID of the action. Not available in initialize.
currentSteps	Collection	Current steps of the instance. Not available in initialize.
Store	WorkflowStore	The workflow store.
Descriptor	WorkflowDescriptor	The workflow descriptor.

If there is any `register` in the `WorkflowDescriptor`, it is also available in the map with the register name as a key.

Variable Interpolation in the Definition

You might notice a strange ${result} in the code of the last example in Chapter 2. Every time OSWorkflow evaluates the workflow definition, it uses something called variable interpolation to define variable values at run time. For example:

```
...
<unconditional-result old-status="JoinFinished"
                                    status="${result}" step="4" />
...
```

The variable ${result} is resolved to any transient variable in the map with the key as result or any value stored in the `PropertySet` of the instance with the result key. Variables interpolated are always of string type.

The first example used interpolation in an XML attribute like status, but interpolation can also be used in scripts. The following example sends an email with a dynamic header.

```
<function type="class">
  <arg name="class.name">com.opensymphony.workflow.util.SendEmail
  </arg>
  <arg name="to">dnlazo@osde.com.ar
```

```
        </arg>
        <arg name="from">dnlazo@osde.com.ar
        </arg>
        <arg name="subject">Holidays</arg>
        <arg name="cc">dnlazo@osde.com.ar
        </arg>
        <arg name="message">Your request has been ${result}
        </arg>
        <arg name="smtpHost">10.250.0.168
        </arg>
    </function>
```

Variable interpolation is a very useful feature to create complex business processes.

PropertySet and Transient Variables

Business processes need to store bits of data during their lifetime or certain periods of time for working purposes. The data that stays alive only during the workflow instance execution is called transient data. Information stored across invocations is called persistent data.

To address the issue of persistent data OSWorkflow uses an open-source component called PropertySet. PropertySet stores and manages data in a type-safe way and integrates with OSWorkflow storing a set of variables for each Workflow instance.

Exploring PropertySet

PropertySet is another open-source Java component from OpenSymphony. It doesn't differ too much from the classic java.util.Map, with the exception of the persistent capabilities and strong typing features.

You don't need to download anything to use PropertySet inside OSWorkflow; everything you need is bundled with the default distribution; be sure to include the propertyset-1.3.jar in your application's classpath.

Each Workflow instance has a PropertySet instance associated by default. You can use it inside the workflow definition or inside custom functions or conditions. The implicit variable propertySet represents the PropertySet for the Workflow instance in the BeanShell scripting context. You can also access the PropertySet inside FunctionProviders and Conditions code.

PropertySet has several persistence implementations such as JDBC, Hibernate, and a memory-based storage. It also uses different methods to store and retrieve data in a type-safe way, such as get/setString(), get/SetInteger(), etc.

Using the PropertySet to Store Variable Data

The following `WorkflowDescriptor` fragment shows how to use the `PropertySet` assigned to this `Workflow` instance to store a variable:

```
<function type="beanshell">
  <arg name="script">propertySet.setString("foo", "bar")
  </arg>
</function>
```

In this definition snippet, we have stored the value `bar` inside the variable named `foo`. It shows how `PropertySet` behaves just like a typical `java.util.Map` would. It's basically an associative array with keys and values. By knowing the key, we can retrieve the value. As in `java.util.Map`, keys are compared with the `equals` and `hashcode` rules for both retrieving and storing values.

The `PropertySet` has a `set` method for every primitive type, such as `get/setBoolean()` for Boolean, `get/SetByte()` for byte arrays, and so on. `PropertySet` also supports some complex types such as XML, binary data, and properties objects.

Depending on the configuration of the `PropertySet` component, this variable may or may not be stored persistently.

If this `PropertySet` implementation supports a persistent store (such as JDBC or Hibernate), this value of `foo` is stored until you remove it or clear the entire `PropertySet`. On the other hand if your implementation is volatile like the memory-backed `PropertySet`, this value is cleared every time your JVM restarts.

Using the PropertySet to Retrieve Stored Data

Having stored a value, the next logical thing would be to be able to retrieve it at a later time. The following `WorkflowDescriptor` fragment shows the retrieval of the same variable:

```
<function type="beanshell">
  <arg name="script">
  System.out.println(propertySet.getString("foo"))
  </arg>
</function>
```

This BeanShell function prints the contents of variable `foo` to the console. If there's no value with the key `foo`, the `PropertySet` returns `null`, just like a `java.util.Map`. If we don't know the type at compile time, we can use the old `get` method. If we call the wrong method for the variable's type, `PropertySet` will try to convert the value to the method you called; that is, if you called `getInteger()` on a string value you'll get the string's integer value or an exception if it's not possible.

Cleaning the PropertySet

You can remove a single value or clear all the values from the `PropertySet`. To remove a single value, use the `remove(String key)` method with the key of the value as the parameter. To clear all the values from the `PropertySet`, call the `remove()` method without any parameter.

Configuring the PropertySet

To configure the `PropertySet` you need the `propertyset.xml` file in the application classpath. This file is loaded when you first call the `PropertySet` and it defines the persistence mechanism to be used along with other configuration options for the specific `PropertySet` implementation. A sample `propertyset.xml` file is as follows:

```xml
<propertysets>
    <propertyset name="jdbc" class="com.opensymphony.module.propertyset
                                    .database.JDBCPropertySet">
    <arg name="datasource" value="jdbc/DefaultDS"/>
    <arg name="table.name" value="OS_PROPERTYENTRY"/>
    <arg name="col.globalKey" value="GLOBAL_KEY"/>
    <arg name="col.itemKey" value="ITEM_KEY"/>
    <arg name="col.itemType" value="ITEM_TYPE"/>
    <arg name="col.string" value="STRING_VALUE"/>
    <arg name="col.date" value="DATE_VALUE"/>
    <arg name="col.data" value="DATA_VALUE"/>
    <arg name="col.float" value="FLOAT_VALUE"/>
    <arg name="col.number" value="NUMBER_VALUE"/>
    </propertyset>
</propertysets>
```

Several `PropertySet` implementations can be defined in the `propertySet.xml` file, each with different names. In this example, we have configured the JDBC implementation `com.opensymphony.module.propertyset.database.JDBCPropertySet` with the name `jdbc`.

By default, this `PropertySet` uses a JDBC datasource configured in the first `arg` element. The other elements can be used to fine-tune the configuration by setting different values such as table and column names. These values for tables and columns are the default for the SQL scripts delivered with the OSWorkflow distribution. The DDL scripts needed for the persistent `PropertySet` can be found inside the OSWorkflow SQL scripts. It consists of only one table called `OS_PROPERTYENTRY`.

PropertySet is not searchable in the sense of an RDBMS, so if you need to search for domain data in your application, you will need to use a standard approach—create a database for the domain objects and attach a workflow identifier to each domain object. This will enable you to do a powerful search of the domain data and refer to the Workflow instance when needed.

PropertySet is useful for storing little pieces of data, and is not suitable for the persistence of our application's main domain objects such as invoices, customer contacts, or forms.

Adding Code to our Definition

This section is about customizing and adding functionality to our XML OSWorkflow process definition. Both classic Java code and BeanShell scripts are available to extend and enhance the business process.

FunctionProviders

During execution and transitioning of the workflow instance you may need to execute code specific to your application or custom functionality. OSWorkflow provides a way to do so, through the use of FunctionProvider.

The FunctionProvider can be a regular Java class, an EJB, or a BeanShell script. OSWorkflow has several useful built-in functions that you can use in your definition.

Creating our first FunctionProvider

Defining a Java FunctionProvider is very easy; all you need to do is implement the com.openshymphony.workflow.FunctionProvider interface. A sample FunctionProvider that simply prints its arguments is shown in the following code snippet:

```
package packtpub.osw;

import java.util.Map;

import com.opensymphony.module.propertyset.PropertySet;
import com.opensymphony.workflow.FunctionProvider;
import com.opensymphony.workflow.WorkflowException;

public class PrintFunction implements FunctionProvider
{
    public void execute(Map transientVars, Map args, PropertySet ps)
```

```
                      throws WorkflowException
  {
     System.out.println(args);
  }
}
```

The execute() method receives the classic transientVars map, the arguments map, and the PropertySet instance. So, inside the FunctionProvider you have access to the workflow entry, the context, and other useful data. The arguments map contains the argument names and values from the descriptor after every variable interpolation.

The only thing left to complete our first FunctionProvider is defining it in the WorkflowDescriptor. A sample XMLWorkflowDescriptor will include the following elements:

```
<pre-functions>
  <function type="class">
    <arg name="class.name">com.opensymphony.workflow.util.Caller
    </arg>
  </function>
</pre-functions>
```

The pre-functions element signals OSWorkflow that the following FunctionProviders will be executed prior to entering the step or the action. The pre-functions element will be the same in step and action-level functions. As you can imagine OSWorkflow also contains the post-functions element, which is executed after leaving the step or action.

Nested within the pre-functions element is the function element. You can have as many functions defined inside the pre-functions as you want. As this is a Java FunctionProvider, the function type attribute is class and the argument is the full qualified name of the Java class to be executed. You can add as many arguments as you want. Note that variable interpolation is active in this case too.

OSWorkflow also supports BeanShell as a quick way to embed code into the workflow definition for quick prototyping. The following example shows a BeanShell action—pre-function. It writes a log line to console, showing the current calling user of the workflow instance:

```
<pre-functions>
  <function type="beanshell">
    <arg name="script">
              System.out.println("Caller is:" + context.getCaller());
    </arg>
  </function>
</pre-functions>
```

As we have seen in the regular Java class `FunctionProvider`, you have to define a pre-`functions` element and a `function` element as well. This time the function type attribute is `beanshell` and its first argument is the BeanShell script code.

We won't cover the EJB `FunctionProviders` as they are difficult to implement and are needed only on a few occasions. If you really need them, then consult the OSWorkflow documentation and examples.

FunctionProvider Types

Depending on the location inside the definition, the `FunctionProviders` are executed at different moments. The following table shows the different types of functions that you can define in OSWorkflow:

	Pre	Post
Action	Executed before the action.	Executed after the action.
Step	Executed *before* the workflow enters the step.	Called prior to the workflow leaving the step.

If you want more in-depth knowledge about the usage of `FunctionProvider`, then look in the OSWorkflow distribution for more examples.

Defining a Custom Function Provider

You can define a custom function either with a Java class or with a BeanShell script. BeanShell is a Java framework that enables scripting into a JVM. It parses and executes a block of Java code. In order to code Java class functions, simply implement the `FunctionProvider` interface in your class:

```
package com.packtpub.osw;

import com.opensymhony.workflow.FunctionProvider;

public class TestFunction implements FunctionProvider
{
void execute(Map transientVars, Map args,
                 com.opensymphony.module.propertyset.PropertySet ps)
{
System.out.println("Hello world.");
}
}
```

Now in order to call the function inside the definition, you have to put the fully qualified class name into the `class.name` argument and set the function type to `class` as shown in the following snippet:

```
<function type="class">
  <arg name="class.name">com.packtpub.osw.TestFunction
  </arg>
</function>
```

This tells the engine to load the `com.packtpub.osw.TestFunction` class, cast it to a `FunctionProvider` interface, and then invoke the `execute()` method.

 Take special care when writing a `FunctionProvider`. It is the most time consuming part of OSWorkflow execution and a major source of trouble when it comes to debugging.

If your function has to receive arguments, you can set the parameter `name` in the function element and its value in the element body. The following fragment shows the same function being invoked with a parameter called `message` and having a value of `Hello OSWorkflow`.

```
<function type="class">
  <arg name="class.name">com.packtpub.osw.TestFunction
  </arg>
  <arg name="message">Hello OSWorkflow
  </arg>
</function>
```

When you call a `FunctionProvider` this way, you must have a way to get the parameters from the `execute()` method. To retrieve the parameter value, you must invoke the `get(Object key)` method of the `args` map. This is shown in the following snippet:

```
package com.packtpub.osw;

import com.opensymhony.workflow.FunctionProvider;

public class TestFunction implements FunctionProvider
{
void execute(Map transientVars, Map args,
                com.opensymphony.module.propertyset.PropertySet ps)
{
System.out.println(args.get("message"));
}
}
```

The `TestFunction` gets the value of the parameter called `message` and prints it to the console. You can receive any data type this way, and not just strings.

Arguments are subject to variable interpolation too. The following fragment uses the same parameter name `message`, but this time the message is `Hello ${employeeName}`. This indicates the engine to parse the string and look for an attribute named `employeeName` inside the workflow instance data (`PropertySet`, transient variables, or inputs).

```
<function type="class">
  <arg name="class.name">com.packtpub.osw.TestFunction
  </arg>
  <arg name="message">Hello ${employeeName}
  </arg>
</function>
```

`FunctionProvider` is a very powerful extension mechanism of OSWorkflow, which brings the power of Java code to our process definitions. This, however, has the drawback of the programming, compiling, and debugging cycle.

BeanShell Scripting

OSWorkflow supports BeanShell scripting within the process definition. The BeanShell project (`http://www.beanshell.org/`) allows the execution of Java code in a script. Conditions, registers, validators, and functions can be defined with BeanShell. A BeanShell script is Java code embedded in the definition like this:

```
<function type="beanshell">
  <arg name="script">true
  </arg>
</function>
```

BeanShell offers a very flexible and useful alternative to traditional Java.

Built-in Functions

There are some built-in utility functions such as `SendMail`, `SendJMSMessage`, `Caller`, etc. as shown in the following table:

Function	Description
Caller	Sets the transient variable "caller" to the current user executing an action.
EJBInvoker	Generic EJB Invoker function.
JMSMessage	Sends out a JMS TextMessage to a specified Queue or Topic

Function	Description
LogRegister	This is a register that helps logging using commons-logging.
MostRecentOwner	Sets the transient variable "mostRecentOwner" to the owner of the most recent step that had an ID equal to one of the values in the stepId list.
ScheduleJob	Schedules a job in the Quartz job scheduler to be executed one or more times in the future.
SendEmail	Sends an email to a group of users.
UnscheduleJob	Unschedules a job that was scheduled previously.
WebWorkExecutor	Executes a WebWork function and restores the old ActionContext when finished (but does not provide chaining support yet).
XWorkExecutor	Executes an XWork function

For example to send an asynchronous JMS Message you can reuse the following snippet into your definition:

```
<function type="class">
<arg name="class.name">com.opensymphony.workflow.util.JMSMessage
</arg>
<arg name="queue-factory-location">java:/comp/env/jms/qcf
</arg>
<arg name="queue-location">java:/comp/env/jms/q1
</arg>
<arg name="text">You request has been ${result}
</arg>
</function>
```

Remember that strings enclosed in ${} are interpolated variables from the inputs, transient variables, or PropertySet variables.

Conditions

conditions represent process flow logic; that is, every decision on the business process can be represented with a condition. OSWorkflow allows conditions on results, calling them conditional results. conditions can be nested to make complex conditions, evaluating each condition with AND or OR.

Here is an example of a simple BeanShell condition using AND:

```
<conditions type="AND">
  <condition type="beanshell">
    <arg name="script">true
    </arg>
  </condition>
</conditions>
```

This example script just returns true, so when combined with AND logic it evaluates to true.

Consider the following example with OR:

```
<conditions type="OR">
  <condition type="beanshell">
    <arg name="script">true</arg>
  </condition>
  <condition type="beanshell">
    <arg name="script">false</arg>
  </condition>
</conditions>
```

This `condition` will evaluate to true due to the OR operator.

`conditions` can be used in conditional result and inside actions. If used inside `actions`, they are called `restrictions`.

The following table describes some useful built-in `conditions` along with their parameters.

Built in Condition	Description
StatusCondition	Simple utility condition that returns true if the current step's status is the same as the required argument "status".
OSUserGroupCondition	Simple utility class that uses OSUser to determine if the caller is in the required argument "group".
IsUserOwnerCondition	A simple utility condition that returns true if the current user (caller) is the step owner.

`conditions` are classes that must return a value that equates to true or false. It is possible to implement nested conditions by simply specifying additional `conditions` child elements under a `conditions` element.

Creating our own Condition

To create your own `condition`, your class must implement the `com.opensyhmphony.workflow.Condition` interface. The interface consists of only one method, namely `passesCondition(Map transientVars, Map args, PropertySet ps)`.

```
package packtpub.osw;
import java.util.Date;
import java.util.Map;

import com.opensymphony.module.propertyset.PropertySet;
import com.opensymphony.workflow.Condition;
```

```
import com.opensymphony.workflow.WorkflowException;

/**
 * Allows execution if today is not Sunday.
 */
public class TimeCondition implements Condition
{
  public boolean passesCondition(Map transientVars, Map args,
                        PropertySet ps)throws WorkflowException
  {
    Date date = new Date();
    return date.getDay() != 7;
  }
}
```

This `condition` returns true if the day is not Sunday. In the definition it looks like this:

```
<conditions type="AND">
  <condition type="class">
    <arg name="class.name">com.packtpub.osw.TimeCondition
    </arg>
  </condition>
</conditions>
```

We can modify the class to receive the day that has to be blocked as an argument. The `condition` interface expects a map called `args`. Our modified `condition` class is as follows:

```
package packtpub.osw;
import java.util.Date;
import java.util.Map;

import com.opensymphony.module.propertyset.PropertySet;
import com.opensymphony.workflow.Condition;
import com.opensymphony.workflow.WorkflowException;

/**
 * Allows execution if today is not Sunday.
 */
public class TimeCondition implements Condition
{
  public boolean passesCondition(Map transientVars, Map args,
                        PropertySet ps) throws WorkflowException
  {
    Date date = new Date();
    int day = Integer.valueOf
                        ((String)args.get("dayNumber")).intValue();
    return date.getDay() != day;
```

```
    }
 }
```

We have to modify the workflow definition to send another argument to the class:

```
<conditions type="AND">
  <condition type="class">
    <arg name="class.name">com.packtpub.osw.TimeCondition
    </arg>
    <arg name="dayNumber">7
    </arg>
  </condition>
</conditions>
```

As usual we can use variable interpolation on the `dayNumber` argument.

Registers

When using BeanShell scripting inside the process definition, it's common to use three or four objects every time. OSWorkflow makes this easy for us by providing us with registers. Registers are variable registers; every time a process definition is evaluated, the register is called to put a variable in the transient variables map.

Registers are very useful to return an abstract entity associated with the workflow, such as "claim", "contact", etc.

Using the LogRegister

OSWorkflow includes a LogRegister that puts a Commons Logging Logger into context. Registers can take arguments, which can be interpolated too.

```
<registers>
  <register type="class" variable-name="log">
    <arg name="class.name">com.opensymphony.workflow.util.LogRegister
    </arg>
    <arg name="addInstanceId">true
    </arg>
  </register>
</registers>
```

Then to use the Register just use the variable in a BeanShell script or Java Function.

```
<function type="beanshell" name="bsh.function">
  <arg name="script">transientVars.get("log").info("function
                                                      called");
  </arg>
</function>
```

Implementing a Register

To implement your own `register`, implement the `com.opensymphony.workflow.Register` interface.

```
package com.packtpub.osw;

import com.opensymhony.workflow.Register;

public class AbstractEntityRegister implements Register
{
  public Object registerVariable(WorkflowContext context,
                                 WorkflowEntry entry, Map args,
                                 PropertySet ps)
                                 throws WorkflowException
  {
    return EntityManager.getEntity(entry.getId());
  }
}
```

The only method to be implemented is the `registerVariable` method. It returns an `Object` instance of your register variable. This example returns an abstract entity associated with the `Workflow` instance.

Validators

Business processes usually need to validate the input data used to initiate or action upon the `Workflow` instance. OSWorkflow provides the validator mechanism to cover this functionality. You can define as many validators as you want for every action in the process.

OSWorkflow calls the validators in the `doAction()` and `initialize()` (by defining a validator in an initial action) methods.

By simply implementing the `com.opensymphony.workflow.Validator` interface you can code your own validator. Additionally, you can define a validator in BeanShell. This interface consists of only the `validate()` method. This method is called during the initialization of the workflow as well as in every action.

To validate the input data, the `validate()` method must return an `InvalidInputException` if the input is invalid, else end normally. This method receives the `transientVars` map, the validator arguments map, and the `PropertySet` of the instance.

Creating a Customer Identifier Validator

In this section, we will write a custom validator—one that checks for the existence of a customer identifier in the workflow transient variables.

```
package packtpub.osw;

import java.util.Map;
import com.opensymphony.module.propertyset.PropertySet;
import com.opensymphony.workflow.InvalidInputException;
import com.opensymphony.workflow.Validator;
import com.opensymphony.workflow.WorkflowException;

public class CustomerIDValidator implements Validator
{
  public void validate(Map transientVars, Map args, PropertySet ps)
                    throws InvalidInputException, WorkflowException
  {
    if(transientVars.get("customerId") == null) throw new
                    InvalidInputException("Customer Id is needed.");
  }
}
```

A `validator` is defined inside an `action` element, after the `restrict-to` element within a `validators` element. The `validators` element serves as a container for every `validator` of the action.

```
<validators>
  <validator type="class">
    <arg name="class.name">packtpub.osw.CustomerIDValidator</arg>
  </validator>
</validators>
```

BeanShell Validators

You can also define a `validator` in BeanShell:

```
<validators>
  <validator type="beanshell">
    <arg name="script">
    if(transientVars.get("customerId") == null) return new
                    InvalidInputException("Customer Id is needed.");
    </arg>
  </validator>
</validators>
```

A BeanShell `validator` doesn't work by throwing an `InvalidInputException` because of a BeanShell engine limitation. Instead the value returned by the script is taken into account for validation. These rules are out of the scope of this book and are described in detail in the OSWorkflow documentation.

So now, when we try to execute action 2, the `validator` above will be called to validate the input we had specified. So in our test case, if we now add the following lines of code, we will get an `InvalidInputException` thrown, and the action will not be executed.

```
Map inputs = new HashMap();
inputs.put("customerId", new Integer(1234));
workflow.doAction(workflowId, 2, inputs);
```

Shortening the title will result in a successful execution of the action.

Other Useful Descriptor Concepts

In this section we will discuss some useful features of OSWorkflow that will simplify your workflow designs.

Finish Actions

An `action` can be marked as `Finish` if you want to terminate the workflow after executing it. Remember OSWorkflow will implicitly finish the workflow when arriving at a `step` that has no `actions` and therefore no `results`.

```
<step id="4" name="Notify employee">
  <actions>
    <action id="6" name="Notify" finish="TRUE">
      <pre-functions>
...
        <results>
          <unconditional-result old-status="Finished" status=
                                    "Line approval" step="-1" />
        </results>
    </action>
  </actions>
</step>
```

Auto Actions

An action can be defined as auto when you want the engine to execute it automatically when the process arrives at that step. Only one auto action is executed in a step and its conditions evaluate to true. To make an action automatic just set the auto attribute to true; like the code snippet that follows:

```
<step id="4" name="Notify employee">
  <actions>
    <action id="6" name="Notify" auto="TRUE">
      <pre-functions>
...
        <results>
          <unconditional-result old-status="Finished" status=
                                    "Line approval" step="-1" />
        </results>
    </action>
  </actions>
</step>
```

The action with ID 6 will be executed automatically as soon as the business process reaches its fourth step. Auto actions are very useful for process automation and orchestration.

Both Auto and Finish Actions can be used to simplify your definitions and create complex automated business processes.

Summary

This chapter covered PropertySet, a very handy way to store workflow variables, and validators to check the workflow's input data. Also, we introduced advanced definition concepts such as conditions, registers, transient variables, variable interpolation, and BeanShell scripting, for implementing very dynamic business processes. We then took a look at the FunctionProviders.

The next chapter will show you how to embed OSWorkflow into your application and to get the most of the persistence and configuration options. Also, we'll cover the workflow unit testing and the security model of OSWorkflow. Lastly, we will take a brief look at the integration between OSWorkflow and Spring, a very popular lightweight object container.

4
Using OSWorkflow in your Application

As seen in Chapter 2, one way to use OSWorkflow is embedding it into your application. This chapter covers the main API features needed to successfully use OSWorkflow inside your application.

This chapter covers all the details of the OSWorkflow configuration and persistence options. It also talks about unit testing for workflow definitions, which is an indispensable feature for quickly validating and checking descriptors.

We also integrate OSWorkflow with Spring—a popular lightweight object container with features such as declarative transactions and AOP programming. This gives OSWorkflow features to your Spring application.

The chapter ends with OSWorkflow's security mechanisms for restricting access to actions and Workflow instances, and for extending the security model with our own user and group directory such as LDAP.

OSWorkflow Configuration

This section will cover the configuration options available for OSWorkflow. We'll show you how to register the workflow definition created in the previous two chapters and generate new workflow instances through programming. After that, we will see the workflow persistence options offered by OSWorkflow and PropertySet.

Registering our Process Descriptors

Before tackling the aspects of persistence and the workflow factory concept, we must see how we can configure OSWorkflow.

Firstly, the framework configures itself by parsing and reading the `osworkflow.xml` file in the classpath. This file contains several settings, such as the `WorkflowStore` implementation class name, the `WorkflowFactory` handler class name, and so on.

The default `osworkflow.xml` file is as follows:

```
<osworkflow>
  <persistence class="com.opensymphony.workflow.spi.memory
                                          MemoryWorkflowStore"/>
  <factory class= "com.opensymphony.workflow.loader.
                                          XMLWorkflowFactory">
  <property key="resource" value="workflows.xml" />
  </factory>
</osworkflow>
```

OSWorkflow delegates the persistence features—such as loading and saving individual instances—of the engine to an interface named `WorkflowStore`. There are several built-in implementations such as EJB, JDBC, etc. The default `osworkflow.xml` file uses the `MemoryWorkflowStore` implementation for persisting instances in memory.

The `WorkflowFactory` is the interface responsible for reading workflow definitions in any format and giving them to the engine in a proper format. The default implementation is `XMLWorkflowFactory`; obviously this reads XML workflow definitions.

As you can see, the default `osworkflow.xml` file is configured to use an `XMLWorkflowFactory` and points to a resource file called `workflows.xml`. The `workflows.xml` file looks like this:

```
<workflows>
  <workflow name="holiday" type="resource" location="holiday.xml"/>
  <workflow name="loan" type="resource" location="loan.xml"/>
</workflows>
```

The `workflows.xml` file describes which workflow definitions are available and in which file the engine can find the XML data. You can see we have two different processes to initiate—`holiday` and `loan`.

Embedding OSWorkflow into your Application

OSWorkflow can be embedded in any application whether it's J2SE or JEE based by simply including the osworkflow.jar file into the classpath of the application. In any case, you must have the osworkflow.xml file, any referenced resources such as workflows.xml, and the XML of the process in the classpath. In this case, the workflow descriptor name is holiday.xml.

Starting a Workflow

Imagine you have an application that interfaces with OSWorkflow, and you'd like to instantiate a new Workflow. This is as easy as:

```
Workflow wf = new BasicWorkflow("johndoe");
Long id = Wf.initialize("holiday", 1, null);
```

The first line creates a new BasicWorkflow with the current username as parameter. BasicWorkflow objects are heavyweight and it is reasonable to have one instance per user to avoid the creation cost.

The second line executes the initialize() method with the workflow name as the first parameter, the initial action number as the second parameter, and the actions input map as the third parameter. In this case, the workflow name is the definition name as stated in the workflows.xml file. We send null as the third parameter because we need no input parameters to instantiate this particular workflow.

The returned Long is the workflow identification number assigned by the engine. The initial number is defined in the WorkflowDescriptor. If this ID is incorrect, the engine will throw an InvalidActionException.

 This code snippet doesn't call the Configuration object. This is very important if you plan to use differently configured Workflows in the same JVM.

Before initializing a workflow instance, you can test it by calling the Workflow interface method, canInitialize(). If this method returns true, then you can safely execute the initialize() method.

```
boolean canInit = wf.canInitialize("Holiday", 1, null)
```

Executing Actions

We now have a newly created instance; let's execute some actions. We need to invoke the doAction method of the Workflow interface. The code is as follows:

```
Wf.doAction(id, 1, null);
```

The parameters are the workflow identifier number, the action number ID (now you can see why actions must be uniquely numbered within a definition), and a map with inputs for the workflow. We send null as the third parameter indicating that there is no need of external inputs for this workflow type and action.

Every call to the initialize() and doAction() methods takes a map as an input parameter. The transient variables map is merged with this input map, so you can also find the input content. This is the main mechanism to send information to the Workflow instance from the caller. The input map key name is preserved in the transient variables map.

What's the Status?

To get the current steps of the workflow, you must call the getCurrentSteps() method of the Workflow interface. The code snippet is as follows:

```
List steps = wf.getCurrentSteps(id);
```

This method returns a list of StepDescriptor, one for each current step of the Workflow instance. To see the step information, we must call the WorkflowDescriptor. The following code snippet shows you how to do that:

```
for (Iterator iterator = steps.iterator(); iterator.hasNext();)
{
  Step step = (Step) iterator.next();
  StepDescriptor sd = wd.getStep(step.getStepId());
}
```

By iterating the current step list and looking up a StepDescriptor from the WorkflowDescriptor, we can get detailed step information, such as the ID, start date, finish date, and name of the step. If you want to see the history steps, call the getHistorySteps() method. The code is as follows:

```
List steps = wf.getHistorySteps(id);
```

Similarly to its current steps counterpart, getHistorySteps returns a list of StepDescriptor, this time with the completed steps of the Workflow instance. To describe the history steps, you can use the code snippet mentioned earlier to describe the current steps.

What can I Do?

Typically in user interfaces, you must see the actions available for the current steps and the current user. The `Workflow` interface has a method called `getAvailableActions()` for that purpose. The following code fragment shows how to invoke it:

```
int[] actions = wf.getAvailableActions(id, null);
```

The parameters are the workflow instance identifier and the parameters map again. For some action to show as available, it must satisfy some condition such as the existence of external data. The passing of the map allows for this sort of scenario to happen. The method returns an array of action IDs. To retrieve the action names, you must use the `WorkflowDescriptor`. See the following snippet:

```
WorkflowDescriptor wd =
                    wf.getWorkflowDescriptor(wf.getWorkflowName(id));
for (int i = 0; i < actions.length; i++)
{
   String name = wd.getAction(actions[i]).getName();
}
```

The code iterates over the action ID array and calls the `getAction()` descriptor method. This method returns an `ActionDescriptor` — an object that describes an action in the definition. Finally, it calls the `ActionDescriptor.getName()` method to obtain the name of the action.

The Useful Abstract States

Besides the current status and old status values you provide in the definition, OSWorkflow has the concept of an abstract state, which is a state every workflow has implicitly. These states are as follows:

State	Description
Activated	Workflow is live.
Completed	Workflow has been finished without any problem.
Created	Workflow has been initialized but no actions have been executed yet.
Killed	Workflow has been canceled.
Suspended	Workflow has been suspended.
Unknown	The state of the workflow is unknown.

Programmatically you can know the abstract state for a particular `Workflow` instance by calling the `getEntryState()` method.

```
int abstract = wf.getEntryState(long id)
```

You can change the abstract state of the instance by calling the `changeEntryState()` method of the `Workflow` interface. Be sure to check the abstract state constants present in the `Workflow` interface.

Querying the Workflow Store

Human-oriented BPMS have GUIs that let the user realize tasks and search for work items. OSWorkflow permits searching the workflow store via a `WorkflowExpressionQuery`. This class is a GOF composite design pattern, so you can nest expressions into expressions for complex queries.

> This search is a very generic one including only the fields in OSWorkflow. For more powerful searches, you should create a domain concept that can be attached to the workflow ID. For example, the `holiday` workflow uses the domain concept of an Employee Request.
>
> You should have an Employee Request table with all the important domain data, such as department, dates, etc. This is the table to be searched when domain data is needed. If you can survive with only the workflow default data, the following search is very useful.

The following code example searches the store for `Workflows` having current steps with the `OWNER` equal to `johndoe`. Don't worry about the owner; we'll see this concept in the security section of this chapter.

```
WorkflowExpressionQuery q = new WorkflowExpressionQuery
                           (new FieldExpression(FieldExpression.OWNER,
                           FieldExpression.CURRENT_STEPS,
                           FieldExpression.EQUALS, "johndoe"));
List wfs = wf.query(q);
```

The following fields are available for searching:

Field	Description
ACTION	The action that triggered the transition to the step.
CALLER	The caller of the action.
DUE_DATE	The due date of the step.
FINISH_DATE	The finish date of the step. It is Null if the step is not yet finished.
OWNER	The owner of the step.
START_DATE	The start date of the step.
STATE	The state of the workflow.
STATUS	The status of the step.
STEP	The step.
NAME	The name of the business process.

The contexts are as follows:

Context	Description
CURRENT_STEPS	The current steps of the workflow
ENTRY	The workflow entry that is the header information
HISTORY_STEPS	The history steps of the workflow

The operators are as follows:

Operator	Description
EQUALS	Equals operator
GT	Greater than operator
LT	Less than operator
NOT_EQUALS	Not Equals operator

The workflow store drains performance from transactional activity, so use it with care. Some workflow stores don't support querying while others don't support nested expressions; so be sure to check your store. For example, the `HibernateStore` included in OSWorkflow currently doesn't support nested expressions.

Querying the Workflow Factory

The `WorkflowFactory` interface has the following methods to inspect the available workflows descriptors.

The `getWorkflowName()` method returns the workflow name of a particular `Workflow` instance. The `getWorkflowNames()` method returns an array of strings with all the available workflow definition names. Check the following snippet for the usage of these methods:

```
String wfName = workflow.getWorkflowName(workflowId);
System.out.println("available workflows:" +
                        Arrays.toString(workflow.getWorkflowNames()));
```

This code is needed when there's more than one `WorkflowDescriptor` in your system and you want to programmatically query their names. Once you have their names, you can instantiate new workflows or inspect their descriptors.

Inspecting the Workflow Descriptor from Code

The XMLWorkflowDescriptor describes a business process in a human-readable format. When OSWorkflow parses and validates the XML, it builds a memory structure called the WorkflowDescriptor. This descriptor has all the information that the process engine needs to follow the process and to create a new instance of the Workflow. We can get a hold of the descriptor of any factory-registered Workflow by calling the getWorkflowDescriptor() method of the Workflow interface. The following code fragment shows a sample invocation:

```
WorkflowDescriptor wd = wf.getWorkflowDescriptor("holiday");
```

This code will return an object representation of the XML workflow descriptor that we built in Chapter 2. By traversing the descriptor, we can analyze the process structure and get the steps, actions, results, etc. of the WorkflowDescriptor.

 Don't confuse the WorkflowDescriptor with its instances.

You can also build a WorkflowDescriptor programmatically; it is useful for dynamic on-the-fly processes.

Using the Workflow Configuration Object

The examples of instantiating a new workflow that have been discussed so far didn't make any reference to the Configuration object. If you don't call the Configuration object, OSWorkflow assumes a unique configuration for workflows in the JVM. If you plan to use workflows with different store and factory options, you must call the Configuration object. The following code fragment shows you how:

```
Workflow workflow = new BasicWorkflow("Holiday");
Configuration config = new DefaultConfiguration();
workflow.setConfiguration(config);
```

It is recommended to call the Configuration object for flexibility. Be sure to call the setConfiguration method of the Workflow interface to use the per-instance configuration model.

Workflow Interface Implementations

OSWorkflow offers great extensibility by giving us different implementations of the `Workflow` interface. The following table summarizes the relevant features of each one:

Implementation	Features
BasicWorkflow	Basic implementation. It doesn't support transactions.
OfBiz	Based on OfBiz, it supports local transactions.
EJBWorkflow	Using JTA and CMP, it supports global XA transactions. It must be used only inside J2EE-compliant application servers, like JBoss.

The `OfBiz` implementation is based on the transaction components of the OfBiz suite (an open-source ERP) to implement local transactions i.e., JDBC transactions. Use it only if you are storing the `Workflow` instance data in a JDBC-compliant database.

On the other hand, the `EJBWorkflow` alternative will use the JTA J2EE API to create a global transaction in each method invocation, causing an unnecessary overhead for simple applications. Use it only if you need distributed transactions, i.e. a workflow action and another database inserted in one transaction.

Implementations supporting transactions like `OfBiz` and `EJBWorkflow` can roll back the current transaction by calling the `setRollbackOnly()` method. Also, in the case of an exception, OSWorkflow will roll back the current transaction to preserve data consistency.

To change your current implementation just instantiate the implementation class instead of `BasicWorkflow`.

 Remember that `BasicWorkflow` doesn't support transactions!

If none of the options suits your needs, you can create your own `Workflow` class by implementing the `Workflow` interface.

Loading the Descriptors—the Workflow Factory

As we have seen before, OSWorkflow delegates the responsibility of loading workflow definitions to a `WorkflowFactory` implementation. There are three built-in implementations to choose from, namely, `XMLWorkflowFactory`, `JDBCWorkflowFactory`, and `SpringHibernateWorkflowFactory`.

Don't confuse the `WorkflowFactory` with the `WorkflowStore`. The first one manages the descriptors while the latter manages the workflow instance data.

`XMLWorkflowFactory` loads the process definition from an XML file in the file system. This is the default implementation. It takes only one parameter called `resource`, which specifies the `workflow` XML file name. This file is loaded from the classpath. A slightly modified variation is the `SpringWorkflowFactory`, which looks up the XML files from a Spring resource.

Loading Descriptors from a Database

`JDBCWorkflowFactory` uses the database to load the workflow descriptors. This is done with a `BLOB` or `LONG VARCHAR` column. To use this factory, you must declare it in `osworkflow.xml` file; it takes a mandatory parameter called `datasource`, which an is the JNDI name of the JDBC datasource to be used. See the following `osworkflow.xml` file:

```
<osworkflow>
  <factory class=
              "com.opensymphony.workflow.loader.JDBCWorkflowFactory">
    <arg name="datasource" value="jdbc/Defaultds"/>
  </factory>
</osworkflow>
```

This sample file will try to look up a JNDI resource called `jdbc/Defaultds` and then try to get a connection from it. Finally, it will try to use a database table named `OS_WORKFLOWDEFS` to find the workflow descriptors. This table is composed of two columns, the first `WF_NAME`, which is the workflow name and is of the `CHAR` or `VARCHAR` type while the second column is `WF_DEFINITION`. The whole XML will be stored in this column as a `BINARY` or `TEXT` type.

`SpringHibernateWorkflowFactory` is the same as above, but uses the Hibernate framework, benefiting from caching and the high-performance ORM features.

Each `WorkflowFactory` retrieves a `WorkflowDescriptor`, a class representing the structure of the definition in an object-oriented way. Implementing your own `WorkflowFactory` enables you to build workflow definitions on the fly. You can implement a template definition and customize it on the fly using some rules.

You can build your own implementation if none of the options fits your requirement by implementing the `WorkflowFactory` interface.

Persisting Instance Information

OSWorkflow delegates the responsibility of loading and storing instance data to the `WorkflowStore`. Later in the section we'll see the different built-in alternatives. First, we'll take a look at exactly which data is made persistent.

The data that is made persistent in OSWorkflow when you use one of the database-backed alternatives is as follows:

- Workflow entry: The instance header data, such as process name, abstract state, etc.
- Current and history steps: The steps that were travelled and the one that the workflow is in.
- PropertySet: The persistent instance-specific data.

The following figure displays the relationships between them.

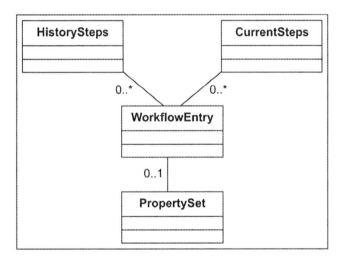

OSWorkflow gives several choices for storing this information. It's very important that you chose your strategy carefully for maintenance and performance reasons. You can configure the persistence strategy in the `osworkflow.xml` file.

Persistence Choices

The following are the built-in `WorkflowStore` implementations in OSWorkflow:

Memory Store

This store strategy saves the workflow information in RAM, useful for testing your business processes.

JDBC

This uses plain old JDBC to access and save the data. It lacks the caching and fetching strategies of Hibernate. The JDBC store is a more basic strategy than Hibernate and is suitable only for very simple workflow applications.

Hibernate

The Hibernate store uses this ORM framework to manage the persistence of `Workflows`. It has the advantage of high performance ORM features such as caching.

Hibernate uses XML files to map objects to relational concepts. In the mapping files, you can tune parameters such as fetching strategies and lazy loading. For more information about Hibernate, take a look at `www.hibernate.org`.

This store is highly recommended as the default production store of OSWorkflow.

Other Stores

OSWorkflow is bundled with other store implementations like `MySQLWorkflowStore`, `SerializableStore`, `OfBizStore`, and `EJBStore`. Be aware that they are designed for very specific scenarios.

If none of the previous strategies suits your needs, then you can build one by implementing the `WorkflowStore` interface.

Configuring the JDBC Store

In this section, we'll configure the JDBC Store for basic usage. This store expects several configuration parameters in the `osworkflow.xml` file:

```xml
<persistence class=
            "com.opensymphony.workflow.spi.jdbc.JDBCWorkflowStore">
<!-- For jdbc persistence, all are required. -->
  <property key="datasource" value="jdbc/DefaultDS"/>
  <property key="entry.sequence"
                            value="SELECT nextVal('seq_os_wfentry')"/>
  <property key="entry.table" value="OS_WFENTRY"/>
  <property key="entry.id" value="ID"/>
  <property key="entry.name" value="NAME"/>
  <property key="entry.state" value="STATE"/>
  <property key="step.sequence"
                            value="SELECT nextVal('seq_os_currentsteps')"/>
  <property key="history.table" value="OS_HISTORYSTEP"/>
  <property key="current.table" value="OS_CURRENTSTEP"/>
  <property key="historyPrev.table" value="OS_HISTORYSTEP_PREV"/>
  <property key="currentPrev.table" value="OS_CURRENTSTEP_PREV"/>
  <property key="step.id" value="ID"/>
  <property key="step.entryId" value="ENTRY_ID"/>
```

```
        <property key="step.stepId" value="STEP_ID"/>
        <property key="step.actionId" value="ACTION_ID"/>
        <property key="step.owner" value="OWNER"/>
        <property key="step.caller" value="CALLER"/>
        <property key="step.startDate" value="START_DATE"/>
        <property key="step.finishDate" value="FINISH_DATE"/>
        <property key="step.dueDate" value="DUE_DATE"/>
        <property key="step.status" value="STATUS"/>
        <property key="step.previousId" value="PREVIOUS_ID"/>
    </persistence>
```

The most important configuration setting is the JNDI datasource, in this case `jdbc/Defaultds`. You must use the same name that you've used to configure the application server's datasource.

The other parameters map the tables, column names, and sequences to be used with the JDBC-backed store. If you didn't modify the included SQL scripts, then these values will work right out of the box. Then you should take a look at the `entry` and `step` sequences, which vary a lot across database vendors.

 Search for SQL scripts tailored to different databases in the `src\etc\ deployment\jdbc` directory.

After you have executed the SQL script and configured the `osworkflow.xml` file, all the new `Workflow` instance and associated data will be stored in the database.

PropertySet Persistence

If you're going to use the `PropertySet` functionality within your `WorkflowDescriptor` and you want to persist the variables, then you must configure the `PropertySet` to use the database instead of the system's memory.

You can configure the `PropertySet` persistence mechanism in the `propertyset.xml` file in the classpath. If you are using a JDBC-based store for persisting instance data, then you should use the `PropertySet`'s counterpart, the `JDBCPropertySet`. As you might have guessed, it stores the `PropertySet` data in a couple of database tables.

Configuring the JDBC PropertySet

Here is the configuration (`propertyset.xml`) to use a JDBC-based `PropertySet`:

```
<propertysets>
    <propertyset name="jdbc" class=
        "com.opensymphony.module.propertyset.database.JDBCPropertySet">
        <arg name="datasource" value="jdbc/DefaultDS"/>
```

```
        <arg name="table.name" value="OS_PROPERTYENTRY"/>
        <arg name="col.globalKey" value="GLOBAL_KEY"/>
        <arg name="col.itemKey" value="ITEM_KEY"/>
        <arg name="col.itemType" value="ITEM_TYPE"/>
        <arg name="col.string" value="STRING_VALUE"/>
        <arg name="col.date" value="DATE_VALUE"/>
        <arg name="col.data" value="DATA_VALUE"/>
        <arg name="col.float" value="FLOAT_VALUE"/>
        <arg name="col.number" value="NUMBER_VALUE"/>
    </propertyset>
</propertysets>
```

This snippet is self-descriptive and includes the usual JNDI datasource name, the table, and each of the column names.

Unit Testing your Workflow

After constructing and changing your business processes, you will want to validate the functionality and flow. This section explains how to use the JUnit framework to verify the correctness and completeness of your business process. This verification is called *unit testing*.

What is JUnit?

JUnit is a unit-testing framework for Java. JUnit is based on a `TestCase` concept: each `TestCase` contains a set of assertions; if any of these assertions fail, the `TestCase` fails. To run unit tests you need to download JUnit from `http://junit.org/index.html`. Unpack the distribution and copy `junit.jar` to your classpath; that's the only file we need to run our example (in addition to the OSWorkflow libraries we've used before).

For this example, we'll build a JUnit `TestCase` with a set of assertions about the current steps and available actions of a sample `WorkflowDescriptor`. You can extend this example with your own set of assertions, as they vary across business processes. Here's the `TestCase` code:

```
package packtpub.osw;

import java.util.Collection;
import java.util.HashMap;
import junit.framework.TestCase;
import com.opensymphony.workflow.Workflow;
import com.opensymphony.workflow.basic.BasicWorkflow;
import com.opensymphony.workflow.config.Configuration;
import com.opensymphony.workflow.config.DefaultConfiguration;
import com.opensymphony.workflow.spi.Step;
```

```java
/**
 * Basic workflow testcase
 */
public class WorkflowTestCase extends TestCase
{
  private Workflow workflow;
  private long workflowId;
    /** Creates a workflow instance for testing. **/
    public void setUp()
    {
      final String wfName = "holiday2";
      workflow = new BasicWorkflow("test");
      Configuration config = new DefaultConfiguration();
      workflow.setConfiguration(config);
      try
      {
        workflowId = workflow.initialize(wfName, 100, new HashMap());
      } catch (Exception e)
        {
          e.printStackTrace();
        }
    }

    public void testWorkflow()
    {
      try
        {
          int[] availableActions =
                    workflow.getAvailableActions(workflowId,null);
          assertEquals("Unexpected number of available actions", 1,
                                        availableActions.length);
          assertEquals("Unexpected available action", 1,
                                        availableActions[0]);
          Collection currentSteps =
                            workflow.getCurrentSteps(workflowId);
          assertEquals("Unexpected number of current steps", 1,
                                        currentSteps.size());
          Step currentStep = (Step) currentSteps.iterator().next();
          assertEquals("Unexpected current step", 1,
                                        currentStep.getStepId());
        } catch (Exception e)
          {
            e.printStackTrace();
            fail();
          }
    }
}
```

The `setup()` method is the first thing to be executed by JUnit by convention. Our test extends from `TestCase` as every JUnit test does, and the `testWorkflow()` method is the one executed by the framework after the `setup()` method. All methods that start with the name "test" will be executed as part of the `TestCase`. In the `testWorkflow()` method, you'll notice several `assertEquals` invocations; these are the JUnit assertions. For example, take the following block of code:

```
int[] availableActions =
            workflow.getAvailableActions(workflowId,null);
assertEquals("Unexpected number of available actions", 1,
                                availableActions.length);
assertEquals("Unexpected available action", 1,
                                availableActions[0]);
```

First, we will query the available actions of the `Workflow` instance, which we created in the `setUp()` method. Then, we will test the assertion of the number of available actions (in this case, it's just one) and the identifier of the available action (in this case, 1).

The second block checks that the new instance is in exactly one current step and this step has the identifier 1:

```
Collection currentSteps =
                    workflow.getCurrentSteps(workflowId);
assertEquals("Unexpected number of current steps", 1,
                                currentSteps.size());
Step currentStep = (Step) currentSteps.iterator().next();
assertEquals("Unexpected current step", 1,
                                currentStep.getStepId());
```

Finally in the catch block, there's one `fail()` method to cancel the test if anything goes wrong.

```
} catch (Exception e)
{
    e.printStackTrace();
    fail();
}
```

When we are done with coding the unit test, it's time to run it, and verify the assertion, thus validating the user requirements about the business process.

Running the Tests

The JUnit testing framework is made up of only one JAR file, `junit.jar`. To run the `TestCase`, you must have this JAR in your classpath and must execute the following command:

```
C:\org.junit_3.8.1>java -cp junit.jar;osworkflow-2.8.0.jar;
commons-logging.jar;
propertyset-1.4.jar
            junit.textui.TestRunner.packtpub.osw.WorkflowTestCase;
```

This command will invoke the JUnit default `TestRunner` on our `packtpub.osw.WorkflowTestCase`. `TestRunner` is a class responsible for executing each `TestCase` and returning the success or failure code of each one. JUnit has several `TestRunners`, some text-based and others graphical. Refer to the JUnit documentation for more details.

The output of the previous command is as follows:

```
C:\org.junit_3.8.1>java -cp junit.jar;osworkflow-2.8.0.jar;
commons-logging.jar;
propertyset-1.4.jar
            junit.textui.TestRunner.packtpub.osw.WorkflowTestCase;
Time: 0,25
OK (1 test)
C: \org.junit_3.8.1>
```

The `TestRunner` tells us that the test finished OK with no failures. This indicates that the process definition is complete enough to cover all the user requirements. You should run this unit test every time you make changes to the business process descriptor. This assures that the requirements are fulfilled and serves as a regression testing.

Integrating with Spring

In this section we'll discuss the integration of OSWorkflow with the Spring lightweight object container.

Spring is an object container, specifically an **Inversion of Control (IoC)** container. IoC containers manage their component's dependencies and lifecycle. Component dependencies are managed declaratively via injection. This way each component only knows its dependency interface but not its implementation. The implementation is the one instantiated by the container and set to the component as an interface, so you don't need to create new object dependencies inside your code. This means no more use of the `new` keyword in Java.

The Object Registry—BeanFactory

Spring uses the concept of a BeanFactory. This BeanFactory is an application-wide registry and manages components. It is responsible for instantiating and injecting objects and their dependencies.

OSWorkflow can be integrated with the Spring container as a bean in the BeanFactory. In this way you can declaratively manage OSWorkflow dependencies.

In addition to this native integration, OSWorkflow can utilize Spring-managed beans for `Functions`, `Conditions`, and other components.

The current Spring version supported by OSWorkflow is 2.0. To download the Spring Framework, go to `www.springframework.org`. To include Spring in your application, just put the `spring.jar` file in the classpath. For each module you use, several different third-party libraries are required; in this example, only the `hibernate3.jar` file is needed.

The Spring BeanFactory's beans are usually defined in an XML file called `BeanFactory.xml`. This file must reside in the classpath and contains each bean and its dependencies declarations. A sample `BeanFactory.xml` file is as follows:

```xml
<?xml version="1.0" encoding="UTF-8"?>
<!DOCTYPE beans PUBLIC "-//SPRING//DTD BEAN//EN"
                "http://www.springframework.org/dtd/spring-beans.dtd">
<beans>
  <bean id="Employee" class="packtpub.osw.Employee">
    <property name="salary">
      <value>1000</value>
    </property>
  </bean>
</beans>
```

The `beans` tag is the root element of the XML; all `bean` tags must be nested inside it. The `bean` tag declares a new bean inside the BeanFactory. The `id` attribute serves as a unique identifier inside the BeanFactory and the `class` attribute marks the Java class to be instantiated by reflection.

The `property` tag tells Spring to set a value to the JavaBean `name` attribute, in this case `salary`. The `value` element nested inside the `property` tag defines the value to be set, in this case `1000`. This value can be converted automatically by Spring, depending on the type of the target JavaBean `property`.

 Note that the Spring convention is to create only once instance per component—a singleton model. To override this behavior, you must set the bean element's `singleton` attribute to false.

OSWorkflow includes a sample `BeanFactory.xml` named `osworkflow-spring.xml` along with its distribution to show how to incorporate OSWorkflow functionality into your Spring-based application. This file lacks a Hibernate `SessionFactory`, so it's not functional out of the box. It's important to understand each bean in this file, so let's go fragment by fragment:

```
<bean id="workflowStore" class=
                        "com.opensymphony.workflow.spi.hibernate.
                                SpringHibernateWorkflowStore">
    <property name="sessionFactory">
      <ref bean="sessionFactory"/>
    </property>
</bean>
```

The first bean is the `WorkflowStore`. Its implementation, the `SpringHibernateWorkflowStore` uses Hibernate for persistence and joins the current Spring transaction by default. It has one mandatory JavaBean `property` to be set, which is the Hibernate 3 `SessionFactory`.

After the `WorkflowStore` bean, comes the `SpringWorkflowFactory` that extends the default `XMLWorkflowFactory` and enables the loading of the configuration directly from the container. The definition is as follows:

```
<bean id="workflowFactory" class="com.opensymphony.workflow.loader.
                        SpringWorkflowFactory" init-method="init">
    <property name="resource">
      <value>workflows.xml</value>
    </property>
    <property name="reload">
      <value>true</value>
    </property>
</bean>
```

You will notice an `init-method` attribute. This tells Spring to call the method with the same name as the attribute immediately after creating the bean, in this case the `init` method. The following fragment below shows the definition of the `SpringConfiguration`:

```
<bean id="osworkflowConfiguration" class=
                "com.opensymphony.workflow.config.SpringConfiguration">
    <property name="store">
      <ref local="workflowStore"/>
    </property>
    <property name="factory">
      <ref local="workflowFactory"/>
    </property>
</bean>
```

Remember that the Configuration interface plays a coordination role between the WorkflowStore (which manages instance data) and the WorkflowFactory (which loads the template definitions). So it's natural to see the two mandatory properties of the SpringConfiguration, a WorkflowStore and a WorkflowFactory. The two previous bean definitions are referenced using the ref element.

Lastly, you must let Spring manage the Workflow implementation of your choice. In the following code snippet, we will define the BasicWorkflow implementation.

```
<bean id="workflow" class="com.opensymphony.workflow.basic.
                              BasicWorkflow" singleton="false">
  <property name="configuration">
    <ref local="osworkflowConfiguration"/>
  </property>
</bean>
```

Note that the bean definition is a prototype one, that is, a bean with the singleton attribute set to false. It is created every time your code calls the BeanFactory and requests the workflow bean. This is a very important concept for you to grasp: Spring creates only one instance of each bean by default.

The two JavaBean properties are the configuration (mandatory) and the typeresolver (optional).

Lastly, we will add a Hibernate SessionFactory declaration to the XML:

```
<bean id="dataSource" class=
      "org.springframework.jdbc.datasource.DriverManagerDataSource">
    <property name="driverClassName">
      <value>org.hsqldb.jdbcDriver</value>
    </property>
    <property name="url">
      <value>jdbc:hsqldb:data/osworkflow</value>
    </property>
    <property name="username">
      <value>sa</value>
    </property>
    <property name="password">
      <value></value>
    </property>
</bean>

<bean id="sessionFactory" class=
      "org.springframework.orm.hibernate3.LocalSessionFactoryBean">
    <property name="dataSource">
      <ref local="dataSource"/>
    </property>
```

```
      <property name="mappingResources">
        <list>
          <value>com/opensymphony/workflow/spi/hibernate3/
                                HibernateCurrentStep.hbm.xml</value>
          <value>com/opensymphony/workflow/spi/hibernate3/
                                HibernateHistoryStep.hbm.xml</value>
          <value>com/opensymphony/workflow/spi/hibernate3/
                                HibernateWorkflowEntry.hbm.xml</value>
        </list>
      </property>
      <property name="hibernateProperties">
        <props>
          <prop key="hibernate.dialect">
          org.hibernate.dialect.HSQLDialect
          </prop>
        </props>
      </property>
    </bean>
```

This creates a new Hibernate `SessionFactory` available to the `WorkflowStore` defined in the first fragment. But before we declare a `SessionFactory`, we must define a datasource (in this case using the HSQL database) on which the OSWorkflow instance data resides; this is the purpose of the `dataSource` bean.

The `SessionFactory` defines some Hibernate mapping files (using the `list` element) included with OSWorkflow to map the `entry` and `step` objects to the corresponding tables.

This definition is not currently included in the OSWorkflow distribution, and you must manually merge the `osworkflow-spring.xml` file with it.

Using our BeanFactory

Once the XML of the `BeanFactory` has been set up, you can invoke OSWorkflow functionality inside your Spring application. The following code snippet shows you how:

```
package packtpub.osw;

import java.util.Collections;
import org.springframework.beans.factory.xml.XmlBeanFactory;
import org.springframework.core.io.ClassPathResource;
import com.opensymphony.workflow.Workflow;

public class SpringExample
```

```
{
  public static void main(String[] args)
  {
    XmlBeanFactory beanFactory =new XmlBeanFactory(
    new ClassPathResource("osworkflow-spring-hibernate3.xml");
    Workflow workflow = (Workflow) beanFactory.getBean("workflow");
    try
    {
      workflow.initialize("example", 100, null);
    } catch (Exception e)
      {
        e.printStackTrace();
      }
  }
}
```

This example initializes the Spring `BeanFactory`, and then gets a `workflow` bean. Note that the code is using the `Workflow` interface and never calls the actual `BasicWorkflow` implementation. This really decouples our code from the implementation details, leaving more room for the more important things such as business logic.

This code is much simpler than the other versions shown before. You don't have to care about creating or looking up `DataSource`, `OSWorkflow Configuration`, and `SessionFactory` or instantiating new `Workflow` implementations. We also get rid of the `workflows.xml` file by uniting all under the same XML file.

Transaction Support in Spring

Before we use Spring and OSWorkflow in production, we must define some important things such as transactions.

Spring's transaction manager can use different strategies, such as JTA global transactions, JDBC local transactions, or no transactions at all.

 JTA is a standard J2EE API capable of creating and synchronizing transactions across different systems. Most of the popular J2EE application servers, such as JBoss, include a JTA subsystem.

The Spring container can also make use of AOP. AOP is a new programming technique, which simplifies the programming of applications by factoring out cross concerns such as logging code, transaction handling code, etc.

If you need to make use of transactions during use of Workflow instances, then you must include a transactional aspect and weave it into the OSWorkflow code. This weaving is done transparently by the container. The transactional aspect is another bean referencing the OSWorkflow `Workflow` bean. Aspects are also called interceptors.

```
<bean id="transactionInterceptor" class="org.springframework.
                    transaction.interceptor.TransactionInterceptor">
  <property name="transactionManager">
    <ref local="transactionManager"/>
  </property>
  <property name="transactionAttributes">
    <props>
      <prop key="*">PROPAGATION_REQUIRED</prop>
    </props>
  </property>
</bean>

<bean id="workflow" class=
                  "org.springframework.aop.framework.ProxyFactoryBean">
  <property name="singleton">
    <value>false</value>
  </property>
  <property name="proxyInterfaces">
    <value>com.opensymphony.workflow.Workflow</value>
  </property>
  <property name="interceptorNames">
    <list>
      <value>transactionInterceptor</value>
      <value>workflowTarget</value>
    </list>
  </property>
</bean>

<bean id="workflowTarget" class=
    "com.opensymphony.workflow.basic.BasicWorkflow" singleton="false">
  <constructor-arg>
    <value>test</value>
  </constructor-arg>
  <property name="configuration">
    <ref local="osworkflowConfiguration"/>
  </property>
</bean>
```

Now the original bean is substituted by a proxy, which wraps each `Workflow` interface method with transaction handling code (the `TransactionInterceptor` bean). The original `workflow` bean is now called the target bean of the interceptor.

With this addition, the `initialize()` method of the example code block in the previous section would run on its own transaction, due to the `PROPAGATION_REQUIRED` transaction attribute for all the `Workflow` interface methods.

The SpringTypeResolver

By using a `SpringTypeResolver` you can describe the beans that implement the `Function` or other resolver-supported interfaces and reference them by name inside the `WorkflowDescriptor`. To define a resolver, add this bean element to the BeanFactory XML:

```xml
<bean id="workflowTypeResolver"
        class="com.opensymphony.workflow.util.SpringTypeResolver"/>
```

Then, modify the `workflow` bean definition by adding a new `property` element:

```xml
<bean id="workflow"
                class="com.opensymphony.workflow.basic.BasicWorkflow"
                                                singleton="false">
    <property name="configuration">
      <ref local="osworkflowConfiguration"/>
    </property>
    <property name="resolver">
      <ref local="workflowTypeResolver"/>
    </property>
</bean>
```

After that, add a `Function` bean that looks like this in the BeanFactory XML:

```xml
<bean id="SampleBusinessLogicFunction"
        class="com.packtpub.logic.SampleBizLogic" singleton="false" />
```

It can be declared and used in the `WorkflowDescriptor` in the following way:

```xml
<function type="spring">
  <arg name="bean.name">SampleBusinessLogicFunction</arg>
</function>
```

The new "spring" function type signals the `WorkflowDescriptor` to resolve the bean name with the Spring BeanFactory via a call to the `BeanFactory.getBean()` method with the bean name as the method parameter. The `SampleBusinessLogicFunction` would obviously have to implement the classic `FunctionProvider` interface.

The resolver is very useful for decoupling the function definition from the actual function implementation.

This section doesn't try to be a tutorial for Spring. On the contrary it hardly brushes the surface of all Spring features. Refer to the Spring project documentation for more details.

Workflow Security

Every business process defines proper roles for each activity or step; for example only managers can sign a check over 10, 000 dollars, or only the person who initiated the process can finish it by approving or rejecting something.

OSWorkflow makes security very flexible for the programmer by discriminating step permissions and actions restrictions independently, and using the concept of step ownership to assign tasks directly to some users.

In addition to this, OSWorkflow relies on the OSUser open-source component to manage user authentication and authorization. OSUser has very powerful extension mechanisms; but you are not bound to it, OSWorkflow can use any security package by using Conditions for instance.

First we'll cover step permissions, which allow us to define status or group conditions to restrict entering any workflow process step.

Step Permissions

The first and basic security measure is the step permission. The step permission denies or allows entry to the step to the current user by means of one or more Conditions. Let's see an example:

```
<step id="1" name="First Draft">
  <external-permissions>
    <permission name="permA">
      <restrict-to>
        <conditions type="AND">
          <condition type="class">
            <arg name="class.name">
            com.opensymphony.workflow.util.StatusCondition
            </arg>
            <arg name="status">Underway</arg>
          </condition>
          <condition type="class">
```

```
            <arg name="class.name">
            com.opensymphony.workflow.util.AllowOwnerOnlyCondition
            </arg>
          </condition>
        </conditions>
      </restrict-to>
    </permission>
  </external-permissions>
      <actions>
  ...
  </step>
```

The `external-permissions` element is applicable inside the `step` element. It contains one or more named permissions, which are restrictions nesting conditions. These conditions are evaluated; if they are true, the user has permission, otherwise the user cannot enter the step. Also, if the permission fails, the user has no available actions from that step.

In this example, if the workflow status is `Underway` and the owner is invoking the process, the permission predicate evaluates to true, enabling access to the user.

You can query the current permissions needed for the execution of the step by calling the `getSecurityPermissions()` method, which receives the workflow identifier and an inputs map:

```
List perms = workflow.getSecurityPermissions(workflowId, null);
```

This method returns a `java.util.List` of permission names in string form.

Action Restrictions

Sometimes a lot of users have access to the step, but each role has an action dedicated to it. For securing individual actions there are action restrictions. A restriction is simply a condition that must be met for the user to execute the action. Take a look at the following descriptor snippet:

```
<action id="2" name="Sign Up For Editing">
  <restrict-to>
    <conditions type="AND">
      <condition type="class">
        <arg name="class.name">
        com.opensymphony.workflow.util.StatusCondition
        </arg>
        <arg name="status">Queued</arg>
      </condition>
```

```
        <condition type="class">
        <arg name="class.name">
        com.opensymphony.workflow.util.OSUserGroupCondition
        </arg>
        <arg name="group">bars
        </arg>
        </condition>
    </conditions>
  </restrict-to>
</action>
```

In this example, all the conditions must evaluate to true (AND operator) and the action will became available to the user when getAvailableActions() is called.

Step Ownership

Every step has an attribute called the owner. This attribute is useful for assigning ownership of a step to a user. In this way you can define Conditions that require access to the step owner or you can query the step by its owner.

The owner attribute for the step is set in the result that provoked the transition to it. The owner attribute too is subjected to variable interpolation. The next descriptor fragment shows an unconditional-result that tells the engine to go to step 2 and set the owner of step 2 to the same name as that of the current user:

```
<results>
<unconditional-result old-status="Finished" step="2"
                                            owner="${caller}"/>
</results>
```

Extending User and Group Authentication and Authorization

By default, OSWorkflow will look up an OSUser user object. It also has several built-in conditions to handle this type of users.

```
UserManager um = UserManager.getInstance();
User test = um.createUser("jdoe");
test.setPassword("test");
Group  foos = um.createGroup("foos");
Group  bars = um.createGroup("bars");
Group  bazs = um.createGroup("bazs");

    test.addToGroup(foos);
```

```
            test.addToGroup(bars);
            test.addToGroup(bazs);

        workflow = new BasicWorkflow("jdoe");
```

OSUser has a singleton `UserManager` responsible for managing users and groups. This code snippet creates a user named `jdoe` with a password, and assigns it to three groups.

After that a new workflow is instantiated with the user's name. OSWorkflow automatically binds the OSUser user and his or her built-in user.

For more advanced security requirements and to follow the security architecture your company has you have to extend OSUser. OSUser supports a very large range of pluggable providers for each function:

- **Credentials**: The process of verifying that the user is authentic.
- **Access Control**: This is used for determining whether a user is allowed to perform a certain task.
- **Profile**: This has personal details and data associated with the user.
- **Management**: This allows the underlying data to be modified.

The `osuser.xml` file is the main configuration file for OSUser. Here, you can configure the different built-in pluggable providers or a custom made one.

```
<opensymphony-user>
    <provider class="com.opensymphony.user.provider.memory.
                                        MemoryAccessProvider" />
    <provider class="com.opensymphony.user.provider.memory.
                                        MemoryCredentialsProvider" />
    <provider class="com.opensymphony.user.provider.memory.
                                        MemoryProfileProvider" />
    <authenticator class="com.opensymphony.user.authenticator.
                                        SmartAuthenticator" />
</opensymphony-user>
```

OSUser has built-in providers for LDAP, plain files, UNIX, and Windows NT users, PAM, JAAS, and JDBC.

By using OSUser you can extend the security of OSWorkflow. If none of the security providers suits your needs, you can create a new one or alternatively create a new security mechanism inside OSWorkflow.

Summary

This chapter covered a lot of ground; first we learned how to configure OSWorkflow to load XML descriptors, and then we took a very through view of the OSWorkflow API to use it inside our applications as an embedded workflow engine.

Later we saw the persistence alternatives OSWorkflow has to store the workflow descriptor and instance data. We also saw the JUnit unit-testing framework that allows us to verify the correctness and validate the functional requirements of our business processes.

We saw that Spring enables us to decouple our application with clear separation of concerns and declarative transactions and security. OSWorkflow integrates seamlessly with Spring benefiting from of all it features.

The chapter ended with the description of the different built-in security mechanisms of OSWorkflow such as actions and step restrictions. We also learned how to extend the OSWorkflow user and group directory by using OSUser.

The next chapter is about the JBoss Rules engine, a very efficient way to decouple and reuse the business logic inside our business processes.

5

Integrating Business Rules with JBoss Rules

This chapter introduces Rule Engines and the JBoss Rules open-source rule engine. We show the ability to integrate the JBoss Rules engine into OSWorkflow. This capability eases the implementation of real-world business processes along with complex business rules. We approach the chapter with an example found in the banking domain, a loan-risk process.

Incorporating Business Logic into Business Processes

Each task in a business process can be performed automatically. When a task can be done automatically, it's because the business process has embedded knowledge about the task and can make logical decisions about it. This knowledge can be in the form of program code or another knowledge representation, such as a decision table.

This knowledge about a process is called business logic or business rules. For instance, a business rule in a bank loan process can be 'validate the amount requested versus the amount limit; if it exceeds the amount limit cancel the loan'. All business rules clearly have two parts—the 'if' or condition part, and the 'then' or consequence part. If the condition is true, then the consequence is executed. This structure will be clearer later on in the chapter.

There are two ways to embed this knowledge inside our OSWorkflow business processes, depending on the type of rules. For most simple rules, OSWorkflow `Conditions` are more than enough, but for complex logic a Business Rules Management System is needed. In this chapter we will cover both ways—the `Condition`-based approach and JBoss Rules, an open-source Java Rule Engine designed for the execution and inference of complex and sophisticated rules.

Simple Logic with Conditional Results

Most business processes have a simple logic in the form of decisions: branch points that follow a condition predicate. The `Conditions` construct in OSWorkflow serves as a branch point for workflows with conditional results.

Remember that `Conditions` can be BeanShell scripts or Java classes implementing `com.opensymphony.workflow.Condition`.

In this chapter we'll use an example from the financial domain, a simple loan request processes performed in every bank. This process has been depicted in the following figure.

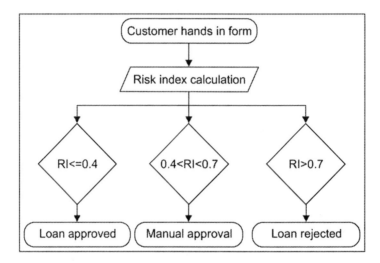

The business process begins when the bank customer hands in the signed loan-application form. This form contains several personal, financial, and employment data such as social security number, loan amount, annual salary, and so on.

This data is used to calculate a risk index (RI) with a loan-risk algorithm. If this index is above a certain threshold the loan is rejected, otherwise it is approved.

This is an oversimplified risk index calculation algorithm for loans from a typical bank:

- Annual Earnings
  - If annual earnings > amount requested, then risk A= 0.0
  - If annual earnings >= 50% amount requested, then risk A= 0.5
  - If annual earnings < 50% amount, then risk A = 1.0

- Previous Credit History
  - ○ If previous credit is paid, then risk B = 0.0
  - ○ If previous credit is unpaid, then risk B = 0.5
  - ○ If there is a legal situation, then risk B = 1.0
- Marital Status
  - ○ If single, then risk C = 0.5
  - ○ If married, then risk C = 0.0
- Final Risk Index = (risk A + risk B + risk C)/3

If the final risk index is below 0.4, then the loan is approved automatically as the risk involved is low. If the index is between 0.4 and 0.7, then a manual approval or rejection is needed. If the index is over 0.7, then the loan is denied automatically as the risk involved is too high.

All the customer data in the form is passed to OSWorkflow in the form of a `Loan` JavaBean having the following structure:

```
package packtpub.osw;

/**
 * Money Loan Request
 */
public class LoanRequest {
  private float amount;
  private String customerName;
  private boolean married;
  private float annualEarnings;
  private boolean creditHistory;
  private boolean previousCreditPaid;
  private boolean previousLegalSituation;

  ...getters/setters
}
```

An instance of this object is passed on to the inputs map of the `initialize()` and `doAction()` methods. The OSWorkflow XML definition file is as follows:

```
<?xml version="1.0" encoding="UTF-8"?>
<!DOCTYPE workflow PUBLIC "-//OpenSymphony Group//DTD OSWorkflow
2.6//EN" "http://www.opensymphony.com/osworkflow/workflow_2_8.dtd">
<workflow>
  <initial-actions>
    <action id="100" name="Start Workflow">
```

```
        <results>
          <unconditional-result old-status="Finished"
                          status="Customer handles form" step="1" />
        </results>
      </action>
    </initial-actions>
    <steps>
      <step id="1" name="Risk index calculation">
        <actions>
          <action id="1" name="Calculate" >
            <results>
              <result old-status="Calculation FinishedA"
                                  status="Approved" step="2">
                <conditions type="OR">
                  <condition type="beanshell">
                    <arg name="script">
                      <![CDATA[packtpub.osw.LoanRequest lr
                      = (packtpub.osw.LoanRequest)transientVars.get
                      ("loanRequest");System.out.println
                      ("Amount:" + lr.getAmount());
                      float riskA = 0.0f;
                      float riskB = 0.0f;
                      float riskC = 0.0f;
                      if(lr.getAnnualEarnings() > lr.getAmount())
                      {
                        riskA = 0.0f;
                      }else
                      if(lr.getAnnualEarnings() >= (lr.getAmount()/2))
                      {
                        riskA = 0.5f;
                      } else
                      {
                        riskA = 1.0f;
                      }
                      if(lr.hasCreditHistory())
                      {
                        if(lr.getPreviousCreditPaid())
                        {
                          riskB = 0.0f;
                        }else{
                          riskB = 0.5f;
                        }
                        if(lr.isPreviousLegalSituation())
                        {
```

```
                    riskB = 1.0f;
                  }
                }
                if(!lr.isMarried())
                {
                  riskC = 0.5f;
                }
                System.out.println("riskA" + riskA);
                System.out.println("riskB" + riskB);
                System.out.println("riskC" + riskC);
                float finalRisk = ((riskA + riskB + riskC)/3);
                System.out.println("finalRisk:" + finalRisk);
                if(finalRisk < 0.4f)
                {
                  System.out.println("Approved");
                  return true;
                }
                return false;
                ]]>
              </arg>
            </condition>
          </conditions>
        </result>
        <unconditional-result old-status="Calculation Finished"
                              step="2" status="Denied"/>
        </results>
      </action>
    </actions>
  </step>
  <step id="2" name="Risk index calculation done" >
  </step>
  </steps>
</workflow>
```

This is a standard definition consisting of two steps, but the key part of the definition is the conditional result of step one. If the condition is true (the risk index allows automatic approval), then the status of the final step is set to Approved. If the index is high, then the status is set to Denied. The status of the business process is derived from the output of the risk index.

Notice that all the code required to calculate the index is embedded in the definition; we can put it into a Java Class but we will lose dynamicity. Another option available is putting the code into a Rule Engine.

Complex Business Logic

In the previous example, for each business rule, a BeanShell Condition was needed. This can really clutter the definition. To reuse rules and to program more complex logic, we need a more powerful tool. This tool is a **Business Rule Management System (BRMS)**.

BRMS is a component inside a BPMS solution. It emerged out of a need to create, execute, maintain, and organize business logic and rules for use inside and outside business processes. The key part of the BRMS is the rule engine.

A rule engine decouples the business rules from the code and externalizes them outside the code. Each change to a business rule doesn't impact the process definition or the program code. On the other hand, it increases the complexity of the solution.

What is "JBoss Rules"?

JBoss Rules is a Rete-based rule engine. This means that the engine evaluates the condition each time a new fact is introduced in the working memory. A fact is just an object and the working memory is the object scope that the rules are allowed to see. Each rule is composed of a condition and a consequence.

If the condition is true, the consequence is executed. If multiple conditions turn true, then the order of consequence execution is defined by a conflict-resolution strategy. This is better explained in the following figure:

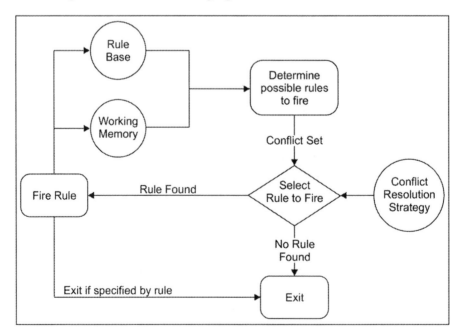

The JBoss Rules architecture is as follows:

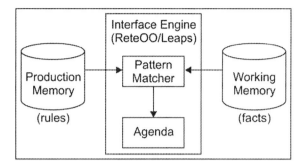

Rules cannot be fired in isolation. Every time you assert an object in the working memory and call the `fireAllRules()` method, the engine will try to match each rule predicate with the working memory contents and all that match will be executed. The rules that match are ordered into an Agenda. This agenda changes every time an object is asserted into the working memory.

This is a clearly a paradigm shift from the procedural approach of regular Java code. This is called a declarative approach to logic. You declare the rules, but the order and activation of the rules depend on the data you input to the engine.

Creating a Rule

JBoss Rules has a proprietary format for rule writing, called DRL. DRLs are simply text files. A JBoss `Rules` rule is an expression of the form:

```
Rule ""
when
    <conditions>
then
    <actions>
end
```

This structure is analogous to:

```
if ( <LHS> ) {
    <RHS>
}
```

LHS and RHS stand for Left Hand Side and Right Hand Side respectively. Each rule has a namespace associated with it called a package. The RHS is standard Java code, but the LHS has a particular syntax, which is described later.

Executing a Rule

Once you have written the rule, the execution is very easy. The following code snippet shows you how:

```
try
{
    PackageBuilder builder = new PackageBuilder();
    builder.addPackageFromDrl(new InputStreamReader(getClass()
                            .getResourceAsStream("/loan.drl")));
```

First, we create a `PackageBuilder` and load the DRL file `loan.drl` from the classpath containing the rules into the builder.

```
    org.drools.rule.Package pkg = builder.getPackage();
    RuleBase ruleBase = RuleBaseFactory.newRuleBase();
    ruleBase.addPackage(pkg);
```

Rules are grouped logically into `RuleBases` (a logical grouping of rules, which are cohesive) and `Packages` (these are compiled and optimized rules files). Thus, we get the package object from the rules file and create a `RuleBase` to execute the rules.

```
    WorkingMemory workingMemory = ruleBase.newWorkingMemory();
    Loan loan = new Loan();
    loan.setAmount(100000);
    FactHandle handle = workingMemory.assertObject(loan);
```

After the rules and packages are loaded, we create a `WorkingMemory` from the `RuleBase`. This `WorkingMemory` stores the transient objects that are within the scope during the execution of rules. You can create as many `WorkingMemories` as you want.

The `Loan` object instantiated is a common JavaBean referenced in the rules and the `Amount` is a simple JavaBean float type property. Once instantiated, we assert the `Loan` into the working memory, thus giving the rules sight of the object. The `handle` object is a reference to the object asserted into the `WorkingMemory`; it's useful for tracking purposes.

```
    workingMemory.fireAllRules();
```

We end by firing the rules. This firing searches for the right rule to execute, taking into account the conflict-resolution strategy.

The complete code fragment is as follows:

```
try
{
    PackageBuilder builder = new PackageBuilder();
    builder.addPackageFromDrl(new InputStreamReader(getClass()
```

```
                                .getResourceAsStream("/loan.drl")));
  org.drools.rule.Package pkg = builder.getPackage();
  RuleBase ruleBase = RuleBaseFactory.newRuleBase();
  ruleBase.addPackage(pkg);
  WorkingMemory workingMemory = ruleBase.newWorkingMemory();
  Loan loan = new Loan();
  loan.setAmount(100000);
  FactHandle handle = workingMemory.assertObject(loan);
  workingMemory.fireAllRules();
}
catch (Exception e)
{
  e.printStackTrace();
}
```

Integrating with OSWorkflow

JBoss Rules integration with OSWorkflow is performed by a `Condition` and a `FunctionProvider`. `Condition` gives the rules the flow of control of the process; the `FunctionProvider` simply executes rules at a designated moment.

RulesCondition

The `RulesCondition` is like any other OSWorkflow `Condition` and implements `com.opensymphony.workflow.Condition`. The helper object `RuleConditionalResult` is available in every rule set executed through the `Condition` to mark the return value of the `Condition` predicate. The return value of the condition is the `RuleConditionalResult.getResult()` result.

Also, the `transientVars` and arguments map contents are passed directly to the JBoss Rules `WorkingMemory`.

The only mandatory parameter of the `Condition` is the `ruleName`. This parameter indicates which DRL file from the classpath will be loaded and executed.

You can append other parameters in the invocation, which will be available as objects inside the `WorkingMemory`. Remember that variable interpolation is also applicable.

```xml
<?xml version="1.0" encoding="UTF-8"?>
<!DOCTYPE workflow PUBLIC "-//OpenSymphony Group//DTD OSWorkflow
2.6//EN" "http://www.opensymphony.com/osworkflow/workflow_2_8.dtd">
<workflow>
  <initial-actions>
    <action id="100" name="Start Workflow">
      <results>
```

```
                <unconditional-result old-status="Finished"
                              status="Customer handles form" step="1" />
          </results>
        </action>
    </initial-actions>
    <steps>
      <step id="1" name="Risk index calculation">
        <actions>
          <action id="1" name="Calculate" >
            <results>
              <result old-status="Calculation FinishedA"
                                        status="Approved" step="2">
                <conditions type="OR">
                  <condition type="class">
                    <arg name="class.name"packtpub.osw.RuleCondition
                    </arg>
                    <arg name="ruleName">/loan.drl
                    </arg>
                  </condition>
                </conditions>
              </result>
              <unconditional-result old-status=
                    "Calculation Finished"step="2" status="Denied" />
          </results>
        </action>
      </actions>
    </step>
    <step id="2" name="Risk index calculation done" >
    </step>
   /steps>
</workflow>
```

Clearly, this definition is smaller and cleaner. We have decoupled the business logic for the index calculation and put it in an external rule file. Even if the algorithm changes, the process definition remains untouched.

The code for the custom JBoss Rules `Condition` is very small:

```
package packtpub.osw;

import java.util.Iterator;
import java.util.Map;

import org.drools.WorkingMemory;

import com.opensymphony.module.propertyset.PropertySet;
```

```
import com.opensymphony.workflow.Condition;
import com.opensymphony.workflow.WorkflowException;

/**
 * Drools Condition
 */
public class RuleCondition implements Condition
{
  public boolean passesCondition(Map transientVars, Map args,
                        PropertySet arg2) throws WorkflowException
  {
    WorkingMemory wm = DroolsHelper.setupRules
                                  ((String)args.get("ruleName"));
    RuleConditionalResult result = new RuleConditionalResult();
    for (Iterator iter = transientVars.values().iterator();
                                            iter.hasNext();)
    {
      wm.assertObject(iter.next());
    }
    wm.assertObject(result);
    wm.fireAllRules();
    System.out.println("Condition:" + result.getResult());
    return result.getResult();
  }
}
```

It uses a `DroolsHelper` to load the DRL file and instantiate a `WorkingMemory`. Then it puts all the contents of the `transientsVars` map into the working memory along with an instance of the `RuleConditionalResult` class. Finally, it fires the rules returning the Boolean result of the `RuleConditionalResult` instance.

The following code is the helper return holder, the `RuleConditionalResult`:

```
package packtpub.osw;

/**
 * Holder of rule result for conditions.
 */
public class RuleConditionalResult{
    private boolean result;

    /**
     * @return the result
     */
    public boolean getResult() {
        return result;
```

```
        }

        /**
         * @param result the result to set
         */
        public void setResult(boolean result) {
            this.result = result;
        }

}
```

It's just a holder for a `boolean` primitive. A third helper class used in conjunction with the JBoss Rules `FunctionProvider` and `Condition` is the `DroolsHelper`.

```
package packtpub.osw;

import java.io.InputStreamReader;

import org.drools.RuleBase;
import org.drools.RuleBaseFactory;
import org.drools.WorkingMemory;
import org.drools.compiler.PackageBuilder;

/**
 * Helper for JBoss Rules integration.
 */
public class DroolsHelper
{
    private static WorkingMemory workingMemory;
    public static WorkingMemory setupRules(String ruleFile)
                    {
        try
        {
          PackageBuilder builder = new PackageBuilder();
          builder.addPackageFromDrl(new InputStreamReader
          (DroolsHelper.class getResourceAsStream(ruleFile)));
          org.drools.rule.Package pkg = builder.getPackage();
          RuleBase ruleBase = RuleBaseFactory.newRuleBase();
          ruleBase.addPackage(pkg);
          workingMemory = ruleBase.newWorkingMemory();
        }catch (Exception e)
        {
                e.printStackTrace();
        }
        return workingMemory;
    }
}
```

It does all the work of loading the DRL file, adding a `Package` to a `RuleBase`, and instantiating a new `WorkingMemory` for them. Finally, the DRL file for the risk index calculation (almost the same as the previous BeanShell implementation) is as follows:

```
package LoanRequestRules;
rule "Calculate"
    when
        lr: packtpub.osw.LoanRequest();
        result: packtpub.osw.RuleConditionalResult();
    then
        System.out.println( "loan" + lr);
        System.out.println("Amount:" + lr.getAmount());
    double riskA = 0.0;
    double riskB = 0.0;
    double riskC = 0.0;

    if(lr.getAnnualEarnings() > lr.getAmount())
    {
      riskA = 0.0;
    }else
    if(lr.getAnnualEarnings() >= (lr.getAmount()/2))
    {
      riskA = 0.5;
    } else {
        riskA = 1.0;
    }

    if(lr.hasCreditHistory())
    {
      if(lr.getPreviousCreditPaid())
      {
        riskB = 0.0;
      }else
      {
        riskB = 0.5;
      }
      if(lr.isPreviousLegalSituation())
      {
        riskB = 1.0;
      }
    }

    if(!lr.isMarried()){
        riskC = 0.5;
    }
```

```
System.out.println("riskA" + riskA);
System.out.println("riskB" + riskB);
System.out.println("riskC" + riskC);
double finalRisk = ((riskA + riskB + riskC)/3);

System.out.println("finalRisk:" + finalRisk);
if(finalRisk < 0.4){
  System.out.println("approved");
result.setResult(true);
}
```

```
end
```

After reading the DRL file, you may notice the when structure:

```
when
        lr: packtpub.osw.LoanRequest();
        result: packtpub.osw.RuleConditionalResult();
```

This tells JBoss Rules to search the WorkingMemory for objects of that type and bind them to the variable name before the colons. After binding, the variables become available for use within the then part.

The then part or consequence is just Java code and in this case it is the same code that the workflow definition has.

Predicates can be a lot more complex than that; please refer to the JBoss Rules documentation for the predicate syntax and more examples.

RulesFunctionProvider

The RulesFunctionProvider executes a DRL file without worrying about the return parameters of the rules.

The mandatory parameter ruleName of the FunctionProvider is the same as that of Condition; it tells it which DRL file to load and execute.

```
package packtpub.osw;

import java.util.Iterator;
import java.util.Map;

import org.drools.WorkingMemory;

import com.opensymphony.module.propertyset.PropertySet;
import com.opensymphony.workflow.FunctionProvider;
import com.opensymphony.workflow.WorkflowException;
```

```
/**
 * Rule executing function provider.
 *
 */
public class RuleExecutorFunctionProvider implements FunctionProvider
{
public void execute(Map transientVars, Map args, PropertySet arg2)
                                          throws WorkflowException
{
  WorkingMemory wm = DroolsHelper.setupRules
                              ((String)args.get("ruleName"));
  for (Iterator iter = transientVars.values().iterator();
                                          iter.hasNext();)
  {
    wm.assertObject(iter.next());
  }
  wm.fireAllRules();
  }
}
```

Declarative programming is a new and exciting approach for business rules. It enables a wealth of new opportunities such as **Domain Specific Languages (DSL)**. For more information about JBoss Rules, refer to its documentation.

Summary

In this chapter, we introduced the location of business logic inside our BPM solution—the BRMS. JBoss Rules is a very powerful open-source rule engine and is the main component of a BRMS. We also learned how to implement simpler logic using OSWorkflow's `Conditions`.

Finally, we created a `RulesCondition` and `RulesFunctionProvider` to make decisions and to execute the set of rules inside our workflow definition.

In the next chapter we'll be using Quartz, an open-source job scheduler to enrich our BPMS with powerful task scheduling capabilities.

6
Task Scheduling with Quartz

In this chapter, we will explore the Quartz task scheduler and its integration with OSWorkflow. We will also give a tutorial with Quartz sending events and actions to OSWorkflow. This gives OSWorkflow temporal capabilities found in some business domains, such as call centers or customer care services.

Both people-oriented and system-oriented BPM systems need a mechanism to execute tasks within an event or temporal constraint, for example, every time a state change occurs or every two weeks. BPM suites address these requirements with a job-scheduling component responsible for executing tasks at a given time.

OSWorkflow, the core of our open-source BPM solution, doesn't include these temporal capabilities by default. Thus, we can enhance OSWorkflow by adding the features present in the Quartz open-source project.

What is Quartz?

Quartz is a Java job-scheduling system capable of scheduling and executing jobs in a very flexible manner. The latest stable Quartz version is 1.6. You can download Quartz from `http://www.opensymphony.com/quartz/download.action`.

Installing

The only file you need in order to use Quartz out of the box is `quartz.jar`. It contains everything you need for basic usage. Quartz configuration is in the `quartz.properties` file, which you must put in your application's classpath.

Basic Concepts

The Quartz API is very simple and easy to use. The first concept that you need to be familiar with is the scheduler. The scheduler is the most important part of Quartz, managing as the word implies the scheduling and unscheduling of jobs and the firing of triggers.

A job is a Java class containing the task to be executed and the trigger is the temporal specification of when to execute the job. A job is associated with one or more triggers and when a trigger fires, it executes all its related jobs. That's all you need to know to execute our `Hello World` job.

Integration with OSWorkflow

By complementing the features of OSWorkflow with the temporal capabilities of Quartz, our open-source BPM solution greatly enhances its usefulness. The Quartz-OSWorkflow integration can be done in two ways—Quartz calling OSWorkflow `workflow` instances and OSWorkflow scheduling and unscheduling Quartz jobs. We will cover the former first, by using `trigger-functions`, and the latter with the `ScheduleJob` function provider.

Creating a Custom Job

Job's are built by implementing the `org.quartz.Job` interface as follows:

```
public void execute(JobExecutionContext context) throws
                                            JobExecutionException;
```

The interface is very simple and concise, with just one method to be implemented. The Scheduler will invoke the `execute` method when the trigger associated with the job fires. The `JobExecutionContext` object passed as an argument has all the context and environment data for the job, such as the `JobDataMap`.

The `JobDataMap` is very similar to a Java map but provides strongly typed `put` and `get` methods. This `JobDataMap` is set in the `JobDetail` file before scheduling the job and can be retrieved later during the execution of the job via the `JobExecutionContext`'s `getJobDetail().getJobDataMap()` method.

Trigger Functions

`trigger-functions` are a special type of OSWorkflow function designed specifically for job scheduling and external triggering. These functions are executed when the Quartz trigger fires, thus the name. `trigger-functions` are not associated with an action and they have a unique ID. You shouldn't execute a `trigger-function` in your code.

To define a `trigger-function` in the definition, put the `trigger-functions` declaration before the `initial-actions` element.

```
...
<trigger-functions>
  <trigger-function id="10">
```

```
    <function type="beanshell">
      <arg name="script">
      propertySet.setString("triggered", "true");
      </arg>
    </function>
  </trigger-function>
</trigger-functions>
<initial-actions>
...
```

This XML definition fragment declares a `trigger-function` (having an ID of 10), which executes a beanshell script. This script will put a named property inside the `PropertySet` of the instance but you can define a `trigger-function` just like any other Java- or BeanShell-based function.

To invoke this `trigger-function`, you will need an OSWorkflow built-in function provider to execute `trigger-functions` and to schedule a custom job—the `ScheduleJob FunctionProvider`.

More about Triggers

Quartz's triggers are of two types—the `SimpleTrigger` and the `CronTrigger`. The former, as its name implies, serves for very simple purposes while the latter is more complex and powerful; it allows for unlimited flexibility for specifying time periods.

SimpleTrigger

`SimpleTrigger` is more suited for job firing at specific points in time, such as Saturday 1st at 3.00 PM, or at an exact point in time repeating the triggering at fixed intervals. The properties for this trigger are the shown in the following table:

Property	Description
Start time	The fire time of the trigger.
End time	The end time of the trigger. If it is specified, then it overrides the repeat count.
Repeat interval	The interval time between repetitions. It can be 0 or a positive integer. If it is 0, then the repeat count will happen in parallel.
Repeat count	How many times the trigger will fire. It can be 0, a positive integer, or `SimpleTrigger.REPEAT_INDEFINITELY`.

CronTrigger

The `CronTrigger` is based on the concept of the UN*X Cron utility. It lets you specify complex schedules, like every Wednesday at 5.00 AM, or every twenty minutes, or every 5 seconds on Monday. Like the `SimpleTrigger`, the `CronTrigger` has a start time property and an optional end time.

A CronExpression is made of seven parts, each representing a time component:

Each number represents a time part:

- 1 represents seconds
- 2 represents minutes
- 3 represents hours
- 4 represents the day-of-month
- 5 represents month
- 6 represents the day-of-week
- 7 represents year (optional field)

Here are a couple of examples of cron expression:

0 0 6 ? * MON: This CronExpression means "Every Monday at 6 AM".

0 0 6 * *: This CronExpression mans "Every day at 6 am".

For more information about CronExpressions refer to the following website:

```
http://www.opensymphony.com/quartz/wikidocs/
CronTriggers%20Tutorial.html.
```

Scheduling a Job

We will get a first taste of Quartz, by executing a very simple job. The following snippet of code shows how easy it is to schedule a job.

```
SchedulerFactory schedFact = new
                         org.quartz.impl.StdSchedulerFactory();
Scheduler sched = schedFact.getScheduler();
sched.start();
```

```
JobDetail jobDetail = new JobDetail("myJob", null, HelloJob.class);
Trigger trigger = TriggerUtils.makeHourlyTrigger();
                                          // fire every hour
trigger.setStartTime(TriggerUtils.getEvenHourDate(new Date()));
                                          // start on the next even hour
trigger.setName("myTrigger");
sched.scheduleJob(jobDetail, trigger);
```

The following code assumes a `HelloJob` class exists. It is a very simple class that implements the job interface and just prints a message to the console.

```
package packtpub.osw;
import org.quartz.Job;
import org.quartz.JobExecutionContext;
import org.quartz.JobExecutionException;
/**
 * Hello world job.
 */
public class HelloJob implements Job
{
  public void execute(JobExecutionContext ctx) throws
                                          JobExecutionException
  {
    System.out.println("Hello Quartz world.");
  }
}
```

The first three lines of the following code create a `SchedulerFactory`, an object that creates `Schedulers`, and then proceed to create and start a new `Scheduler`.

```
SchedulerFactory schedFact = new
                            org.quartz.impl.StdSchedulerFactory();
Scheduler sched = schedFact.getScheduler();
sched.start();
```

This `Scheduler` will fire the `trigger` and subsequently the jobs associated with the `trigger`. After creating the `Scheduler`, we must create a `JobDetail` object that contains information about the job to be executed, the job group to which it belongs, and other administrative data.

```
JobDetail jobDetail = new JobDetail("myJob", null, HelloJob.class);
This JobDetail tells the Scheduler to instantiate a HelloJob object
when appropriate, has a null JobGroup, and has a Job name of "myJob".
After defining the JobDetail, we must create and define the Trigger,
that is, when the Job will be executed and how many times, etc.
```

```
Trigger trigger = TriggerUtils.makeHourlyTrigger();
                                        // fire every hour
   trigger.setStartTime(TriggerUtils.getEvenHourDate(new Date()));
                                        // start on the next even hour
   trigger.setName("myTrigger");
```

The `TriggerUtils` is a helper object used to simplify the `trigger` code. With
the help of the `TriggerUtils`, we will create a `trigger` that will fire every hour.
This `trigger` will start firing the next even hour after the `trigger` is registered
with the `Scheduler`. The last line of code puts a name to the `trigger` for
housekeeping purposes.

Finally, the last line of code associates the `trigger` with the job and puts them under
the control of the `Scheduler`.

```
sched.scheduleJob(jobDetail, trigger);
```

When the next even hour arrives after this line of code is executed, the `Scheduler`
will fire the `trigger` and it will execute the job by reading the `JobDetail` and
instantiating the `HelloJob.class`. This requires that the class implementing the job
interface must have a no-arguments constructor.

An alternative method is to use an XML file for declaring the jobs and triggers. This
will not be covered in the book, but you can find more information about it in the
Quartz documentation.

Scheduling from a Workflow Definition

The `ScheduleJob FunctionProvider` has two modes of operation, depending on
whether you specify the `jobClass` parameter or not. If you declare the `jobClass`
parameter, `ScheduleJob` will create a `JobDetail` with `jobClass` as the class
implementing the job interface.

```
<pre-functions>
  <function type="class">
    <arg name="class.name">com.opensymphony.workflow.util.ScheduleJob
    </arg>
    <arg name="jobName">Scheduler Test
    </arg>
    <arg name="triggerName">SchedulerTestTrigger</arg>
    <arg name="triggerId">10
    </arg>
    <arg name="jobClass">packtpub.osw.SendMailIfActive
    </arg>
    <arg name="schedulerStart">true
```

```
      </arg>
      <arg name="local">true
      </arg>
    </function>
  </pre-functions>
```

This fragment will schedule a job based on the `SendMailIfActive` class with the current time as the start time. The `ScheduleJob` like any `FunctionProvider` can be declared as a pre or a post function.

On the other hand, if you don't declare the `jobClass`, `ScheduleJob` will use the `WorkflowJob.class` as the class implementing the job interface. This job executes a `trigger-function` on the instance that scheduled it when fired.

```
  <pre-functions>
    <function type="class">
      <arg name="class.name">com.opensymphony.workflow.util.ScheduleJob
      </arg>
      <arg name="jobName">Scheduler Test
      </arg>
      <arg name="triggerName">SchedulerTestTrigger
      </arg>
      <arg name="triggerId">10
      </arg>
      <arg name="schedulerStart">true
      </arg>
      <arg name="local">true
      </arg>
    </function>
  </pre-functions>
```

This definition fragment will execute the `trigger-function` with ID 10 as soon as possible, because no CronExpression or start time arguments have been specified.

This `FunctionProvider` has the arguments shown in the following table:

Argument	Description	Mandatory
triggerId	ID of the `trigger` function to be executed if no `jobClass` class name is set. If `jobClass` is specified, this argument is ignored.	Yes
jobName	The job name.	Yes
triggerName	The trigger name.	Yes
groupName	The group name to be shared between the trigger and the job.	No

Argument	Description	Mandatory
Username	The user name to be used when executing the `trigger` function.	No
Password	The password to be used when executing the `trigger` function.	No
Jobclass	If this is specified, `ScheduleJob` will use this class when creating `JobDetail`. Otherwise, `ScheduleJob` will create a job with a class `WorkflowJob`, used to execute the `trigger` function with the ID of `triggerId`.	No
schedulerName	The scheduler name to be used.	No
schedulerStart	If this is set to true, `ScheduleJob` will create and start a new scheduler.	No
txHack	Set this parameter to true if you are having problems with deadlocks in transactions.	No
cronExpression	The cron expression. If this argument is set, a `CronTrigger` will be created. Otherwise, a `SimpleTrigger` will be instantiated.	No
startOffset	This is the offset from the time of execution of the `ScheduleJob` function provider to the next job. Default is 0.	No
endOffset	This is the offset from the time of execution of the `ScheduleJob` function provider to the end of the job. Default is no ending.	No
Repeat	The repeat count of the Job. The default can be 0 or `REPEAT_INDEFINITELY`.	No
Repeatdelay	The offset between repetitions.	No

Transactions in Quartz

Excluding a few minor exceptions, Quartz performs the same transactions in a standalone application or inside a full-blown J2EE Container. One of these exceptions is the use of global JTA transactions inside a JTA-complaint container.

To enable the creation of a new JTA transaction or to join to an existing JTA transaction, just set the `org.quartz.scheduler.wrapJobExecutionInUserTransaction` property inside the `quartz.properties` file to `true`. Enabling this parameter allows the Quartz job to participate inside a global JTA transaction. This in combination with a JTA workflow implementation puts the workflow step and the temporal task into one transaction, thus assuring the information integrity.

JobStores

The JobStore interface designed in Quartz is responsible for the persistence and retrieval of all job and trigger data. There are two built-in implementations of the JobStore interface, the RamJobStore and the JDBCJobStore.

The RamJobStore stores the job, trigger, and calendar data in memory, losing its contents after JVM restarts. On the other hand, JDBCJobStore uses the JDBC API to store the same data.

The JDBCJobStore uses a delegate to use specific functions of each database, for example, DB2, PostgreSQL, etc.

The JobStore configuration is located in the `quartz.properties` file. To set the JobStore, add the following line to the configuration file, if you want to use the RamJobStore:

```
org.quartz.jobStore.class = org.quartz.simpl.RAMJobStore
```

The configuration of the JDBCJobStore is a little more complex as it involves datasources, transactions, and delegates:

To use local JDBC transactions, you only need to set the following parameters:

```
org.quartz.jobStore.class = org.quartz.impl.jdbcjobstore.JobStoreTX
org.quartz.jobStore.dataSource = jdbc/defaultDS
```

The `datasource` is your datasource JNDI name.

To use global JTA transactions, you need the following parameters:

```
org.quartz.jobStore.class = org.quartz.impl.jdbcjobstore.JobStoreCMT
org.quartz.jobStore.dataSource = jdbc/defaultDS
org.quartz.jobStore.nonManagedTXDataSource = jdbc/nonTXDatasource
```

This differs from the JDBC transaction mode in its use of a non-JTA managed datasource for internal JobStore use.

For both transaction modes you need to set the database delegate appropriate for your database.

```
org.quartz.jobStore.driverDelegateClass=
                    org.quartz.impl.jdbcjobstore.StdJDBCDelegate
```

The delegates included with Quartz are as follows:

Database	Delegate class
Generic JDBC	`org.quartz.impl.jdbcjobstore.StdJDBCDelegate`
Microsoft SQL Server and Sybase	`org.quartz.impl.jdbcjobstore.MSSQLDelegate`
PostgreSQL	`org.quartz.impl.jdbcjobstore.PostgreSQLDelegate`
Oracle	`org.quartz.impl.jdbcjobstore.oracle.OracleDelegate`
Cloudscape	`org.quartz.impl.jdbcjobstore.CloudscapeDelegate`
DB2 v7	`org.quartz.impl.jdbcjobstore.DB2v7Delegate`
DB2 v8	`org.quartz.impl.jdbcjobstore.DB2v8Delegate`
HSQLDB	`org.quartz.impl.jdbcjobstore.HSQLDBDelegate`
Pointbase	`org.quartz.impl.jdbcjobstore.PointbaseDelegate`

For more detailed configuration options, refer to the Quartz documentation at `http://www.opensymphony.com/quartz/documentation.action`.

Example Application—Customer Support

In this section we will develop an example to show the capabilities of the OSWorkflow-Quartz duo. In every company, the customer plays a central role. If not attended to correctly, he or she can turn around and buy services or products from a competitor. Every company also has a customer support department and a good performance indicator for this department would be the number of customer requests attended to.

Some customer support requests come from mail or web interfaces. Suppose you have an web application that receives customer support requests. A typical customer support process is as follows:

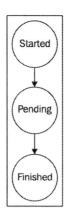

This is the most simple of processes and the most commonly implemented. While in the pending state, the request can be forwarded to many people to finally reach completion. If the request is stalled in this state, the process doesn't add value to the business and doesn't match customer expectations, thereby downgrading the company image and customer loyalty.

So a good approach to the process would be to reduce the percentage of support requests in the pending state. If a support request is in the same state for two hours, an e-mail to the customer support coordinator is send, and if a six hour threshold is exceeded an email is send directly to the customer support manager for notification purposes. These notifications assure the request will never be accidentally forgotten. The decision flow is depicted in the following figure:

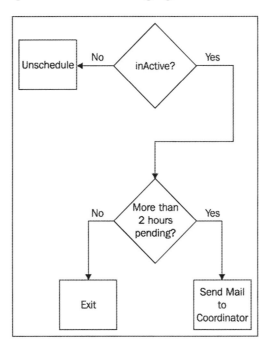

To implement this process logic, we need temporal support in our business process. Obviously this is done by Quartz. The workflow definition is as follows:

```xml
<?xml version="1.0" encoding="UTF-8"?>
<!DOCTYPE workflow PUBLIC "-//OpenSymphony Group//DTD OSWorkflow 2.6
                          //EN" "http://www.opensymphony.com/
                          osworkflow/workflow_2_8.dtd">
<workflow>
  <initial-actions>
    <action id="100" name="Start Workflow">
      <pre-functions>
        <function type="class">
```

```
          <arg name="class.name">packtpub.osw.ScheduleJob
          </arg>
          <arg name="jobName">TwoHourMail
          </arg>
          <arg name="jobClass">packtpub.osw.SendMailIfActive
          </arg>
          <arg name="triggerName">MailIfActive2hTrigger
          </arg>
          <arg name="triggerId">10
          </arg>
          <arg name="schedulerStart">false
          </arg>
          <arg name="local">true
          </arg>
          <arg name="groupName">CustomerSupportJobs
          </arg>
          <arg name="cronExpression">0 0 */2 * * ?
          </arg>
        </function>
        <function type="class">
          <arg name="class.name">packtpub.osw.ScheduleJob
          </arg>
          <arg name="jobName">SixHourMail
          </arg>
          <arg name="jobClass">packtpub.osw.SendMailIfActive
          </arg>
          <arg name="triggerName">MailIfActive6hTrigger
          </arg>
          <arg name="triggerId">10
          </arg>
          <arg name="schedulerStart">false
          </arg>
          <arg name="local">true
          </arg>
          <arg name="groupName">CustomerSupportJobs
          </arg>
          <arg name="cronExpression">0 0 */6 * * ?
          </arg>
        </function>
      </pre-functions>
      <results>
        <unconditional-result old-status="Finished"
                                            status="Pending" step="1" />
      </results>
```

```
        </action>
    </initial-actions>
    <steps>
      <step id="1" name="Pending">
        <actions>
          <action id="1" name="Finish request" finish="true">
            <results>
              <unconditional-result old-status="Finished" step="2"
                                        status="Finished" />
            </results>
          </action>
        </actions>
      </step>
    </steps>
</workflow>
```

So the process definition is very easy, as we have two steps, but the key of the solution lies in the ScheduleJob2 FunctionProvider. This FunctionProvider is a slightly modified version of OSWorkflow's built-in ScheduleJob; the only difference is that the new implementation puts the function provider's arguments in the JobDataMap of the job. The difference from the original ScheduleJob code is as follows:

```
dataMap.putAll(args);
```

There is just one line to put the arguments of the FunctionProvider into the JobDataMap.

The process definition schedules a custom SendMailIfActive job every two hours and a SendMailIfActive job every six hours. If the process is still in pending state, then a mail is sent, otherwise the job is unscheduled. The job code is as follows:

```
package packtpub.osw;
import java.util.Date;
import java.util.Properties;
import javax.mail.Message;
import javax.mail.Session;
import javax.mail.Transport;
import javax.mail.internet.InternetAddress;
import javax.mail.internet.MimeMessage;
import org.quartz.Job;
import org.quartz.JobExecutionContext;
import org.quartz.JobExecutionException;
import org.quartz.SchedulerException;

import com.opensymphony.workflow.Workflow;
```

```java
import com.opensymphony.workflow.basic.BasicWorkflow;
/**
 * Quartz job that send an email if the specified workflow is active.
 */
public class SendMailIfActive implements Job
{
  public void execute(JobExecutionContext ctx) throws
                                        JobExecutionException
  {
    long wfId = ctx.getJobDetail().getJobDataMap()
                                        .getLong("entryId");
    String username = ctx.getJobDetail().getJobDataMap()
                                        .getString("username");
    String to = ctx.getJobDetail().getJobDataMap().getString("to");
    String from = ctx.getJobDetail().getJobDataMap()
                                        .getString("from");
    String subject = ctx.getJobDetail().getJobDataMap()
                                        .getString("subject");
    String text = ctx.getJobDetail().getJobDataMap()
                                        .getString("text");
    String smtpHost = ctx.getJobDetail().getJobDataMap()
                                        .getString("smtpHost");
    String triggerName = ctx.getJobDetail().getJobDataMap()
                                        .getString("triggerName");
    String groupName = ctx.getJobDetail().getJobDataMap()
                                        .getString("groupName");

    Workflow workflow = new BasicWorkflow(username);
    long state = workflow.getEntryState(wfId);
    System.out.println("State:" + state + " for wf:" + wfId);
    if(state != 4)
    {
      sendMail(smtpHost, from, to, subject, text);
    } else
      {
        try
        {
          ctx.getScheduler().unscheduleJob(triggerName, groupName);
        } catch (SchedulerException e)
          {
            e.printStackTrace();
          }
      }
  }
```

```
private void sendMail(String smtpHost, String from, String to,
                                        String subject, String text)
{
  Properties props = new Properties();
  props.put("mail.smtp.host", smtpHost);
  Session sendMailSession = Session.getInstance(props, null);
  try
  {
    Transport transport = sendMailSession.getTransport("smtp");
    Message message = new MimeMessage(sendMailSession);
    message.setFrom(new InternetAddress(from));
    message.setRecipient(Message.RecipientType.TO, new
                                        InternetAddress(to));
    message.setSubject(subject);
    message.setSentDate(new Date());
    message.setText(text);
    message.saveChanges();
    transport.connect();
    transport.sendMessage(message, message.getAllRecipients());
    transport.close();
  } catch (Exception e)
  {
    e.printStackTrace();
  }
}
}
```

This completes the proactive workflow solution commonly requested by users.

Example Application—Claims Processing

Every service organization has a business process to claim for unpaid services. This process is commonly called claim processing. For every unpaid service a new claim is issued to a representative, to contact the customer for payment.

This process is suited for system-oriented BPM, because it's a batch process that goes through every unpaid service, creates a new claim associated with that service, and assigns this claim to a customer representative. This process runs every day and can be represented with an OSWorkflow `workflow` definition. In this `workflow` definition, there's no human intervention; the representative sees only the end result—the customers he or she has to contact.

Additionally this customer contact is a business process in itself, but this time it is a human-oriented business process. The customer representative has a list of customers he or she has to contact each day.

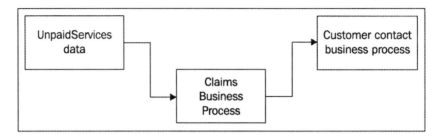

The components of this business solution are as follows:

- A Quartz job that runs every night and creates new instances of the claim processing workflow.

- A `workflow` definition that uses auto-actions and needs no human interaction at all. This definition reflects the real-business process. It gets all the unpaid services from a web service and creates a new customer contact workflow.

- A `FunctionProvider` to call the unpaid services from a web service and create a new customer contact workflow for each one of them.

- A `workflow` definition for the customer contact business process.

By creating a new workflow every day, this workflow is fully automatic and has a little intelligence for identifying failed states.

The first component of the solution is a Quartz job to instantiate a new workflow. We will call this job `WorkflowInitJob`. It is described in the following snippet of code:

```
package packtpub.osw;
import java.util.Map;
import org.quartz.Job;
import org.quartz.JobExecutionContext;
import org.quartz.JobExecutionException;
import com.opensymphony.workflow.Workflow;
import com.opensymphony.workflow.basic.BasicWorkflow;
import com.opensymphony.workflow.config.Configuration;
import com.opensymphony.workflow.config.DefaultConfiguration;
/**
 * Creates a new workflow instance.
 */
public class WorkflowInitJob implements Job
{
    public void execute(JobExecutionContext ctx) throws
```

```
                                        JobExecutionException
{
  String userName = ctx.getJobDetail().getJobDataMap()
                                         .getString("user");
  String wfName = ctx.getJobDetail().getJobDataMap()
                                         .getString("wfName");
  Map inputs = (Map) ctx.getJobDetail().getJobDataMap()
                                         .get("inputs");
  int initAction = ctx.getJobDetail().getJobDataMap()
                                         .getInt("initAction");
  Workflow workflow = new BasicWorkflow(userName);
  Configuration config = new DefaultConfiguration();
  workflow.setConfiguration(config);
  try
  {
    long workflowId = workflow.initialize(wfName, initAction,
                                                    inputs);
    System.out.println("Instantiated new workflow with id:" +
                                            workflowId);
  } catch (Exception e)
    {
      throw new JobExecutionException(e);
    }
  }
}
```

The second component of the claims processing workflow solution is a workflow definition. It is as follows:

```
<?xml version="1.0" encoding="UTF-8"?>
<!DOCTYPE workflow PUBLIC "-//OpenSymphony Group//DTD OSWorkflow 2.6
                          //EN" "http://www.opensymphony.com/
                          osworkflow/workflow_2_8.dtd">
<workflow>
  <initial-actions>
    <action id="100" name="Start Workflow">
      <results>
        <unconditional-result old-status="Finished"
                                          status="Pending" step="1" />
      </results>
    </action>
  </initial-actions>
  <steps>
    <step id="1" name="Get unpaid and create contact">
      <actions>
```

```
        <action id="1" name="process data" finish="true" auto="true">
          <pre-functions>
            <function type="class">
              <arg name="class.name">packtpub.osw
                                      .ClaimsWebServiceProvider
              </arg>
              <arg name="url">http://localhost:8080/ws/unpaid
              </arg>
              <arg name="username">${caller}
              </arg>
            </function>
          </pre-functions>
          <results>
          <unconditional-result old-status="Finished"
                                  step="1" status="Created" />
          </results>
          </action>
        </actions>
      </step>
    </steps>
  </workflow>
```

The customer contact definition is simpler and is as follows:

```
<?xml version="1.0" encoding="UTF-8"?>
<!DOCTYPE workflow PUBLIC "-//OpenSymphony Group//DTD OSWorkflow 2.6
                          //EN" "http://www.opensymphony.com/
                          osworkflow/workflow_2_8.dtd">
<workflow>
  <initial-actions>
    <action id="100" name="Start Workflow">
      <results>
        <unconditional-result old-status="Finished" status="Pending"
                                      step="1" />
      </results>
    </action>
  </initial-actions>
  <steps>
    <step id="1" name="Contact">
      <actions>
        <action id="1" name="Finish contact" finish="true">
          <results>
            <unconditional-result old-status="Finished" step="1"
                                      status="Contacted" />
          </results>
```

```
        </action>
      </actions>
    </step>
  </steps>
</workflow>
```

The third component is a `FunctionProvider`, which calls the unpaid services from a web service and for each unpaid service generates a new customer contact workflow. This `FunctionProvider` uses the Apache Axis Web Service Framework to call a standard SOAP web service. You can find more information about the Apache Axis framework at the following website: `http://ws.apache.org/axis/java/index.html`.

The `FunctionProvider` code is as follows:

```
package packtpub.osw;

import java.util.Iterator;
import java.util.List;
import java.util.Map;

import com.opensymphony.module.propertyset.PropertySet;
import com.opensymphony.workflow.FunctionProvider;
import com.opensymphony.workflow.Workflow;
import com.opensymphony.workflow.WorkflowException;
import com.opensymphony.workflow.basic.BasicWorkflow;
import com.opensymphony.workflow.config.Configuration;
import com.opensymphony.workflow.config.DefaultConfiguration;

/**
 * Gets unpaid services data from web service and
 * creates a new customer contact workflow for each one.
 */
public class ClaimsWebServiceProvider implements FunctionProvider
{
  public void execute(Map arg0, Map arg1, PropertySet arg2)
                                throws WorkflowException
  {
    Workflow workflow = new BasicWorkflow("test");
    Configuration config = new DefaultConfiguration();
    workflow.setConfiguration(config);
    List unpaidData = getUnpaidDataFromWebService();
    for (Iterator iter = unpaidData.iterator(); iter.hasNext();)
    {
      UnpaidService service = (UnpaidService) iter.next();
      Map serviceData = serviceToMap(service);
```

```
        workflow.initialize("customer-contact", 100, serviceData);
    }
  }
  private Map serviceToMap(UnpaidService service)
  {
      ...
  }
  private List getUnpaidDataFromWebService()
  {
      ...
  }
}
```

Finally and to integrate all the solution, there's a Java class designed specifically to call the Quartz `Scheduler` and schedule the Quartz job for running every night.

Quartz has many more features worth exploring. For more information about Quartz check its website and the Quartz Wiki at `http://wiki.opensymphony.com/display/QRTZ1/Quartz+1`.

Summary

In this chapter, we covered the integration of the Quartz job-scheduling system with OSWorkflow, which provided temporal capabilities to OSWorkflow. We also took a look at the `trigger-functions`, which are executed when a Quartz trigger fires. We also learned how to schedule a job from a Workflow definition by using `ScheduleJob`. Finally, we showed the capabilities of the Quartz-OSWorkflow duo with the help of two sample applications.

7
Complex Event Processing

This chapter introduces some state-of-the-art technologies like **Event Stream Processing** (ESP) and **Complex Event Processing** (CEP) and their applications in BPMs. We will look at an OSWorkflow function provider that interfaces with the Esper CEP engine and allows monitoring of real-time process information and events. This chapter assumes basic knowledge of SQL and the relational data model concepts.

Complex Event Processing (CEP)

CEP is a relatively new technology to process events and discover complex patterns inside streams of events. CEP engines are also known as Event Stream Processing (ESP) engines. Events can be anything that happens outside or inside your application. These events contain data about the business situations that occurred and information about the data (also known as metadata). A sequence of events from the same source is called an **event stream**.

By processing the event streams with business-defined patterns, you can detect and react to business situations in real time. For example, you can monitor a financial stock index in real time. If it reaches certain values within an hour, you can react to this by selling a percentage of the stock. The threshold values are defined in a CEP pattern. This pattern tells the CEP engine how to detect and react to this event.

Patterns and Data

CEP technologies use patterns to match events inside the stream and then watch the stream for matches of those patterns. The event stream flows through a pattern chain. If a pattern matches with an event, the engine is notified. This flow of information is the opposite of traditional data handling, such as SQL databases, in which the data is stored and then the patterns (SQL queries) are run over the data to select the relevant data that matches the pattern. This flow is better understood visually.

The following figure displays the event stream as an ongoing flow through which the patterns match the relevant events.

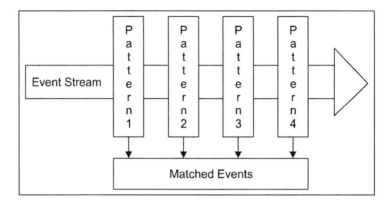

It's common to confuse CEP technology with rule engine technology, such as we saw in Chapter 5. This is because patterns are like rules, in the sense they both have a condition and a consequence.

The difference between the two technologies lies in the temporal component of CEP. This allows the patterns to use time as another dimension. CEP technology enables patterns such as: "select event A if the previous event was B". This would be awkward and difficult to implement in a rule engine. Also, a CEP engine is optimized for real-time or near real-time processing of high volumes of event data.

CEP in BPM

A BPM is an ideal place to implement a CEP engine.

Business events exists naturally in a continuous stream; they happen all the time in the real world and to have a real-time response to them, we must have real-time processing capabilities.

A BPMS naturally identifies its events and it reacts in a manner similar to the workflow—if a sale is closed, the workflow engine will finish this sale workflow instance. So, the event input is provided by all BPM suites. The CEP engine, taking advantage of this event input provided by the BPMS, gives them pattern matching and real-time processing capabilities.

A CEP engine is a new but very useful component of a BPMS and it enables the BPMS to react in real time to relevant business events. Additionally, it provides real-time Business Activity Monitoring to important business situations and especially to business exceptions.

In addition to BPM event processing, real-world uses of CEP include fraud detection, automatic stock trading, SLA and KPI monitoring, and sensor applications (RFID, etc.).

What is Esper?

Esper is an open-source Java CEP engine. Esper, like OSWorkflow needs to be embedded inside your application, it doesn't run in standalone mode. Esper is optimized for the processing of very large volume of events in real time.

The Esper Architecture

This section describes the three most important concepts in Esper architecture: events, patterns, and listeners.

Esper, like every CEP engine analyzes an event stream and detects relevant events, matching them with user-defined patterns. For Esper, these events are regular JavaBeans and the patterns are represented in EQL. EQL is a special language designed for pattern matching and its syntax is very similar to that of SQL.

The patterns in EQL are registered in the Esper engine and when an event arrives, it is checked against all the active patterns. What happens when one or more patterns match the event? The Esper engine notifies the listeners of the event's matching patterns.

This mechanism is analogous to the observer design pattern. This enables a nice decoupling between the event and the event listeners. Each pattern can have many listeners. The listeners are free to do what they want when notified of an event occurrence—they can print the event information, send an email, etc.—as listeners are made of regular Java code. The following figure displays these interactions in an ordered fashion for better understanding.

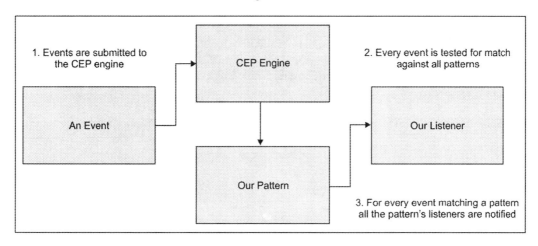

Downloading and Installing Esper

You can download Esper from its web page located at `http://esper.codehaus.org/` and can obtain help and support from the user mailing list. To install Esper, all you need to do is download the Esper distribution and unpack it.

 Esper needs JDK 5 or a higher version to run.

Hello World from Esper

To create our Hello World example we need three things—an event class, a pattern to match events, and a listener to notify when the pattern matches. These basic building blocks are depicted in the following figure:

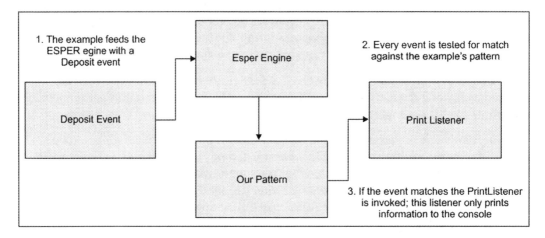

The figure shows these interactions in a numbered sequence. We will first create our event class. Remember that Esper sees events as common POJOs with JavaBean-like properties. This is a very non-intrusive approach; you don't need to couple your application to any Esper API. Additionally, Esper also supports maps and XML elements as events.

A very simple event class is shown in the following code snippet:

```
package packtpub.osw.cep;

/**
 * Sample event class for CEP.
 */
public class Deposit
```

```
{
  private float amount;
  private String customerId;

  /**
  * @return the customerId
  */
  public String getCustomerId()
  {
    return customerId;
  }

  /**
   * @param customerId the customerId to set
   */
  public void setCustomerId(String customerId)
  {
    this.customerId = customerId;
  }

  /**
  * @return the amount
  */
  public float getAmount()
  {
    return amount;
  }

  /**
  * @param amount the amount to set
  */
  public void setAmount(float amount)
  {
    this.amount = amount;
  }
}
```

The Java class shown in this code has two JavaBean properties, namely amount and customerId, and the two respective pairs of JavaBean getters and setters. These properties are handled by Esper using Java's reflection. Next, we need the pattern that the engine will match with the event data. The pattern is just a string containing the following EQL:

```
Every A=packtpub.osw.cep.Deposit
```

This pattern is very simple. It tells the engine that for every arrived event of type `Deposit`, it will notify our listener. The `Every` keyword ensures that Esper will notify not just the first time but every time. No other criterion needs to be matched. The `A=` token pair is a variable assignment and the `packtpub.osw.cep.Deposit` is our JavaBean class name.

Following the pattern, we need the listener. The listener for this example only prints the event information when notified. Listeners need to implement the `net.esper.client.UpdateListener` interface as shown in the `PrintListener` class:

```
package packtpub.osw.cep;

import java.util.Arrays;

import net.esper.client.UpdateListener;
import net.esper.event.EventBean;

/**
 * Simple listener that prints the event to console.
 */
public class PrintListener implements UpdateListener
{
  public void update(EventBean[] newEvent, EventBean[] oldEvent)
  {
    System.out.println(Arrays.toString(newEvent));
  }
}
```

The code shows the `PrintListener` class that implements the `UpdateListener` interface provided by Esper. This listener interface has only one method, the `update()` method, which is invoked when a pattern matches an event occurrence.

This method receives two `EventBean` arrays. The first one is an array of the new events and the other is an array of the events that have already been notified to this listener. Esper stores them in memory, which is known as an event window. You can access this window by using the old events array.

The `EventBean` class is a wrapper class provided by Esper for all type of events.

Finally, to execute the example we need a class with a `main` method, to set up the Esper engine and send it some events. The following code shows this class:

```
package packtpub.osw.cep;

import net.esper.client.EPAdministrator;
import net.esper.client.EPRuntime;
import net.esper.client.EPServiceProvider;
import net.esper.client.EPServiceProviderManager;
```

```java
import net.esper.client.EPStatement;

/**
 * CEP Example test class.
 */
public class CEPTest
{
  public static void main(String[] args)
  {
    EPServiceProvider epService =
                       EPServiceProviderManager.getDefaultProvider();
    EPAdministrator admin = epService.getEPAdministrator();
    EPStatement pattern = admin.createPattern("every A=
                                       packtpub.osw.cep.Deposit");
    PrintListener listener = new PrintListener();
    pattern.addListener(listener);
    Deposit d = new Deposit();
    d.setAmount(100);
    d.setCustomerId("123");
    EPRuntime runtime = epService.getEPRuntime();
    runtime.sendEvent(d);
  }
}
```

The class shown in the code snippet consists of only a main method with all the code needed to set up Esper and a Deposit JavaBean and send it to the engine.

First, it generates an EPServiceProvider, which is an administrative Esper object. From this provider, we get the EPAdministrator and the EPRuntime. The first is responsible for creating patterns and EQL queries, and the second is a gateway to the engine, for passing events to it.

The EPAdministrator.createPattern(String pattern) method generates an EPStatement with the pattern being passed as argument. The EPStatement type is a common superclass for EQL and pattern expression. The registered pattern becomes active right away.

Then our PrintListener is instantiated and associated to the pattern with the EPStatement.addListener(UpdateListener listener) method. The listener becomes active right away. As soon as the pattern matches an event, the update() method of the listener class will be called.

Finally, this class generates a Deposit instance and sends it to the engine via the sendEvent() method of the EPRuntime object. Remember, that our Deposit object is a POJO that also serves as an event for Esper. The pattern is matched every time an object of the class Deposit arrives, so the PrintListener update method is invoked printing the event data to the console.

This is a very simple example but serves as a basic block for any use of Esper inside your applications.

Patterns expressions and EQL

Esper makes the distinction between patterns expressions and EQL queries. Both are enclosed in what Esper calls a statement.

Patterns expressions begin with the keyword `every`, that is, they are activated every time the expression matches an event. EQL queries begin with `select` or `insert` keywords.

The `EPAdministrator.createPattern(String pattern)` and `EPAdministrator.createEQL(String query)` methods both return an instance of an `EPStatement`, a superclass for both pattern expressions and EQL queries.

Push and Pull Mode

The Esper engine supports two usage modes: the push mode and the pull mode. The push mode is like the example we just implemented. The engine notifies (*pushes* to) the listener when an event matching the pattern arrives.

On the other hand, the pull mode queries the engine any time (not only at the time an event arrives) to get the relevant events matching a pattern or query. This mode works by first registering the pull pattern or query in the engine. The pull mode is useful for periodically polling the engine's data and when we are not interested in every pattern match event. The following figure illustrates this mechanism:

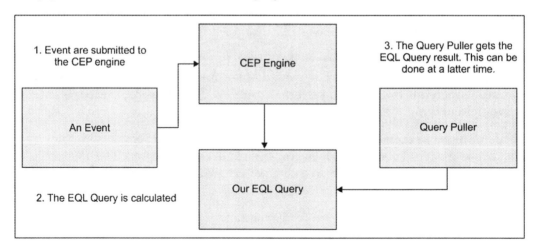

In the figure you can see the Query Puller as the element that retrieves the event data from the EQL Query. Esper allows for both push and pull usage modes with EQL and pattern expressions.

Every `EPStatement` has the `iterator()` method. This method returns a `java.util. Iterator` to be able to visit the pattern or EQL data. This is basically the way the pull mode is implemented in Esper.

Let's modify the example a bit to see how the pull mode works. We'll use the pull mode to ask the engine for the output data of the pattern expression.

The EQL pattern in the following example is the same as before but our test class needs a few changes:

```java
package packtpub.osw.cep;

import java.util.Iterator;

import net.esper.client.*;
import net.esper.event.EventBean;

/**
 * CEP Pull model example.
 */
public class CepCountTest
{
  public static void main(String[] args)
  {
    EPServiceProvider epService =
                        EPServiceProviderManager.getDefaultProvider();
    EPAdministrator admin = epService.getEPAdministrator();
    EPStatement pattern = admin.createPattern("every A=
                                    packtpub.osw.cep.Deposit");
    Deposit d = new Deposit();
    d.setAmount(100);
    d.setCustomerId("123");
    EPRuntime runtime = epService.getEPRuntime();
    runtime.sendEvent(d);
    Iterator<EventBean> it = pattern.iterator();
    System.out.println(it.next().get("A"));
  }
}
```

This time there's no listener registered for the pattern, instead a `EPStatement. iterator()` method is invoked, for which Esper API returns a `java.util.Iterator` with the pulled pattern event data.

When you run this code, it will print the number of times an event of type `Deposit` arrived.

EQL Queries

In the earlier examples, Esper matched the event that arrived with pattern expressions. These expressions are suited for inspection and detection of events; if we want to benefit fully from the CEP technology we must be able to make queries and manipulate the event streams. Esper uses its own proprietary EQL language to both query and handle event streams.

The EQL language is very similar to the SQL standard, especially in the use of the `select` and `insert` statements. But contrary to SQL, the EQL `from` clause applies to event streams and not to relational tables. EQL has several shared characteristics with SQL such as aggregated functions, alias, where conditions, order by statements, etc.

Like the pattern expression, EQL statements, when matched by the engine, call the respective `UpdateListeners` with the event data extracted from the event stream.

For example, the following pattern expression sends an event named A to the `UpdateListener`:

```
Every A=packtpub.osw.cep.Deposit
```

This event named A is of type `Deposit`. When working with EQL queries, the same behavior applies:

```
Select * from packtpub.osw.cep.Deposit
```

This query feeds the whole bean to the `UpdateListener`. The `select` clause must be expressed in the EQL Query; it is not optional. The * symbol after the `select` clause tells Esper to send every property of the bean to the listener. The `from` indicates the event stream from which to get the event data.

This is a very powerful feature. You can join events from different event streams. It is very useful for the BPM engine, as you can have every business process in its own stream, and join them when necessary for complex computations.

Remember that the `EPAdministrator` uses distinct methods for creating pattern expressions (the `createPattern()` method) and EQL queries (the `createEQL()` method). Both methods receive a string parameter containing the pattern expression or the EQL query.

You can specify the engine to get more detailed information as shown in the following EQL query:

```
Select customerId from packtpub.osw.cep.Deposit
```

This query selects only the `customerId` JavaBean property of the `Deposit` beans from the `Deposit` event stream.

What happens if you want to select some but not all events from the event stream? The familiar SQL operator `where` enters in action. The `where` is an optional clause in EQL queries. The following query restricts the events of type `Deposit`, to those that have amounts over 1,000 units.

```
Select customerId from packtpub.osw.cep.Deposit where amount > 1000
```

Esper has a handful of operators available in the `where` clause as shown in the following table:

Operator	Description
=	Equals
<	Less than
>	Greater than
>=	Greater or equal than
<=	Less or equal than
!=	Not
<>	Distinct from
Is null	The expression preceded is null
Is not null	The expression preceded is not null
In	Restricts the range to the values expressed inside the clause
Between	Restricts the range between two values
Like	Restricts the range to values similar to the like expression
Regexp	Restricts the range to values that match the regular expression assigned

EQL also has the alias capability of SQL. For example the first example can be rewritten like this:

```
Select customerId as cId from packtpub.osw.cep.Deposit as d
```

In this EQL query, the `customerId` property is renamed to `cId` and the `Deposit` event stream is named to d. The alias feature is useful for simplifying and shortening queries, making them more readable.

Group By

EQL also supports the `group by` operator. It has the same behavior as that of its SQL counterpart—it groups a column's similar result data into one record:

```
Select customerId, sum(amount) from packtpub.osw.cep.Deposit group by
customerId
```

This EQL query groups the event data by the customer identification number. The listener receives the identification and the sum of all the amounts of each customer. The output of our `PrintListener` is as follows:

```
...
-------------------------
sum(amount):200.0
customerId:1
-------------------------
sum(amount):200.0
customerId:2
-------------------------
sum(amount):200.0
customerId:3
-------------------------
sum(amount):200.0
customerId:4
-------------------------
sum(amount):200.0
customerId:5
-------------------------
sum(amount):200.0
customerId:6
-------------------------
sum(amount):200.0
customerId:7
-------------------------
sum(amount):200.0
customerId:8
-------------------------
sum(amount):200.0
customerId:9
-------------------------
...
```

This query doesn't act over the whole event stream. On the contrary, it groups only one event's data! This is because, as each event arrives, the EQL query is executed upon it. Thus the result is the grouping of just one record, and not of all the records that have arrived so far.

To group a set of events the way SQL does, you must specify an event output rate. To define event output rate in EQL a special and new operator is needed; the `output by` operator serves this purpose.

The following EQL notifies the listener after every two events, thus generating the desired effect:

```
Select customerId, sum(amount) from packtpub.osw.cep.Deposit group by
customerId output every 2 events
```

The EQL's `output every 2 events` clause controls the rate of information sent to the listener. The output is what you may expect:

```
...
sum(amount):100.0
customerId:1
sum(amount):100.0
customerId:2
sum(amount):100.0
customerId:3
sum(amount):100.0
customerId:4
sum(amount):100.0
customerId:5
sum(amount):100.0
customerId:6
sum(amount):100.0
customerId:7
sum(amount):100.0
customerId:8
```

The `PrintListener`'s output shows the grouping of two events each time (this output is rendered with two rounds of identical events).

Time and Event Windows

Esper supports time and event windows for EQL queries and pattern expressions. This enables a very flexible handling of events and supports advanced use cases for CEP. Esper restricts events with time delimiters or event number delimiters.

For example, you can specify an EQL query to have effect over the last four events regardless of the time they arrived. We have modified the previous query:

```
Select customerId, amount from packtpub.osw.cep.Deposit.win:length(4)
```

The window length is defined after the . next to the event stream name. The `win:length(4)` signals Esper to make a window of four events in which the EQL will take effect. Besides event window, you can use a time window.

For example, the following EQL acts on the last four minutes of events regardless of the number of events:

```
Select customerId, amount from packtpub.osw.cep.Deposit.win:time
                                                     (4 minutes)
```

Both time length and event number restrictions support a batch mode, in which the events arrive in a batch to the listener. The previous two examples would look as follows:

```
Select customerId, amount from
                 packtpub.osw.cep.Deposit.win:length_batch(4)

Select customerId, amount from
                 packtpub.osw.cep.Deposit.win:time_batch(4 minutes)
```

The event has an element number parameter and the time has a time period parameter. Examples of time period parameters are as follows:

```
15 seconds
90 minutes 30 seconds
1 day 2 hours 20 minutes 15 seconds 110 milliseconds
```

These examples are self descriptive. The syntax of time windows is as follows:

time-period : [day-part] [hour-part] [minute-part] [seconds-part] [milliseconds-part]

The time and event windows are very useful tools in CEP solutions.

Aggregate Functions

Just like SQL, Esper provides aggregates functions to summarize and perform calculations on the event stream data. The aggregate functions are listed in the following table.

Aggregate function name	Description
sum(expression)	Returns the sum of the values of the expression
avg(expression)	Returns the average of the values in the expression
count(expression)	Returns the number of non-null values in the expression
count(*)	Returns the number of events
max(expression)	Returns the highest value in the expression
min(expression)	Returns the lowest value in the expression
median(expression)	Returns the median value in the expression
stddev(expression)	Returns the standard deviation of the values in the expression
avedev(expression)	Returns the mean deviation of the values in the expression

All aggregate functions listed in this table except count(*) support the distinct modifier. This changes the behavior in some cases. Consult the Esper documentation for more details on the aggregate functions.

This section finishes the EQL and pattern expression overview. For a more in-depth reference to EQL or pattern expressions refer to the Esper official documentation.

Integration with OSWorkflow

This section discusses the Esper integration with OSWorkflow to process business event data and react with user-defined patterns.

Esper Function Provider

To enable Esper functionality inside an OSWorkflow definition, we must create a way to emit events from OSWorkflow into the Esper engine.

OSWorkflow can provide this extension via a custom FunctionProvider. This FunctionProvider will emit events into the engine. The code for the class is as follows:

```
package packtpub.osw.cep;

import java.util.Map;

import net.esper.client.*;

import com.opensymphony.module.propertyset.PropertySet;
import com.opensymphony.util.BeanUtils;
import com.opensymphony.workflow.FunctionProvider;
import com.opensymphony.workflow.WorkflowException;

/**
 * Function provider that sends an event to the esper engine.
 */
public class PushEventFunctionProvider implements FunctionProvider
{
  public void execute(Map transientVars, Map args, PropertySet ps)
                                            throws WorkflowException
  {
    // the event POJO class name to be instantiated by reflection
    String eventClassName = (String) args.get("event.class.name");
    Object event;
    try
    {
      event = Class.forName(eventClassName).newInstance();
```

```
    } catch (Exception e)
      {
        throw new WorkflowException(e);
      }
    //invokes the setters of the event with the argument map data.
    // if a setter name is equals to a map key, it will be called
    // with the key's value as a parameter.
    // f.e.: if the arguemnt Map contains a key "name" with value
    //                                                      "john"
    // and the event bean has a method called setName, it will be
    //                                                     invoked
    // by reflection in the following way: setName("john").
    // See the javadocs for more detail.BeanUtils.setValues(event,
    //                                                args, null);
    // gets the default provider and the default runtime for this
    //                                                        JVM.
    EPServiceProvider epService = EPServiceProviderManager
                                              .getDefaultProvider();
    EPRuntime runtime = epService.getEPRuntime();
    runtime.sendEvent(event);
  }
}
```

This code creates an event of the type passed by the argument to the
`FunctionProvider` and fills its properties with similar matching keys in the
`transientVars` map to send it to the engine. For example, if the bean being
instantiated has a `long` JavaBean property named `amount` and the `transientVars`
map has a similarly named key, the contents (if the type matches) of the key's value
are set into the `amount` property of the JavaBean.

As a regular `FunctionProvider` it can be placed in pre and post functions, in a step
or an action. A snippet of the XML workflow definition is as follows:

```
<post-functions>
  <function type="class">
    <arg name="class.name">packtpub.osw.cep.PushEventFunctionProvider
    </arg>
    <arg name="event.class.name">packtpub.osw.cep.Deposit
    </arg>
    <arg name="amount">${amount}
    </arg>
    <arg name="customerId">${customerId}
    </arg>
  </function>
</post-functions>
```

The `post-functions` element of the snippet has only one function, the `PushEventFunctionProvider` defined in the `class.name` argument as usual. The `amount` and `customerId` argument names are passed to the `FunctionProvider` via the `transientVars` map. Thus ending up in the `event.class.name` (the JavaBean event) specified as `packtpub.osw.cep.Deposit`.

Remember that the `FunctionProvider` arguments are subject to variable interpolation. Finally, a code fragment for testing the functionality of the `FunctionProvider` is as follows:

```
Map inputs = new HashMap();
inputs.put("customerId", "123");
inputs.put("amount", new Float(10000f));
long workflowId = workflow.initialize("cep", 100,
                                        Collections.EMPTY_MAP);
workflow.doAction(workflowId, 1, inputs);
```

This fragment fills an `inputs` map with the `customerId` and `amount` values, and then creates a new workflow of type `cep` and executes action number 1 sending the `inputs` map along. This example assumes you have already set up the Esper engine elsewhere in the code, as well as the patterns and corresponding listeners.

Real-World Examples

This section shows examples of CEP within a BPM environment.

Event-based Mail Alerts

After integration with OSWorkflow, the work that is left to implement the CEP solution over a BPMS is to generate the appropriate patterns and listeners. For example, with a `SendMailListener` we can implement an event-based alert. Additionally, if the pattern is an EQL query, we can use it to mail process performance indicators to a manager in a real-time fashion.

```
package packtpub.osw.cep;

import java.util.Properties;

import javax.mail.Message;
import javax.mail.Session;
import javax.mail.Transport;
import javax.mail.internet.InternetAddress;
import javax.mail.internet.MimeMessage;

import net.esper.client.UpdateListener;
import net.esper.event.EventBean;
```

```
/**
 * This listener send an email with the current data each time
 * in each invocation.
 */
public class SendMailListener implements UpdateListener
{
  private String host;
  private String to;
  private String from;
  private String subject;
  private String bodyPrefix;

  /**
   * Constructor.
   * @param host
   * @param to
   * @param from
   * @param subject
   * @param bodyPrefix
   */
  public SendMailListener(String host, String to, String from, String
                                     subject, String bodyPrefix)
  {
    super();
    this.host = host;
    this.to = to;
    this.from = from;
    this.subject = subject;
    this.bodyPrefix = bodyPrefix;
  }

  public void update(EventBean[] newData, EventBean[] oldData)
  {
    sendMail(host, to, from, subject, bodyPrefix + "\n" + newData);
  }

  private void sendMail(String host, String to, String from, String
                                     subject, String body)
  {
    Properties config = new Properties();
    config.put("mail.host", host);
    Session session = Session.getDefaultInstance(config);
    MimeMessage message = new MimeMessage(session);
    try
    {
      message.addRecipient(Message.RecipientType.TO, new
                                     InternetAddress(to));
      message.addFrom(new InternetAddress[]
```

```
                                              { new InternetAddress(from) });
    message.setSubject(subject);
    message.setText(body);
    Transport.send(message);
  } catch (Exception e)
  {
    e.printStackTrace();
  }
}
}
```

Example 1 — Measuring SLA through KPIs

This example uses Esper as a performance monitor component of a BPMS solution. The aggregate functions such as count, avg, and sum within Esper EQL queries allow a business manager to monitor the **Service Level Agreement (SLA)** of a business process. In this example, we make use of the SendMailListener features.

An SLA in BPMS is defined in terms of the following metrics or KPIs:

- Number of new process instances: Arrival rate per minute
- Completion time of process instances: Completion rate per minute
- Number of errors in process instances: Failure rate per minute

These metrics are sent every minute to a manager by mail. You can easily change this setting by modifying the time. The SLA information is better understood visually, for which a charting feature will be implemented.

Brief Overview of the Example

This example has the following parts:

- Previous section's FunctionProvider
- EQL queries, custom Listener, and SendMailListener
- Charting component

This example uses the FunctionProvider defined in the last section. This FunctionProvider will send events to the Esper engine during the creation, completion, and error steps of a business process. The events will be sent to the registered listeners. There is one event class for each type of event:

1. The ProcessCreationEvent class
2. The ProcessCompletionEvent class
3. The ProcessErrorEvent class.

There is an EQL query for each type of event, calculating the statistics needed for the KPI's values. The same listener is registered for these three. This listener passes the values to the Charting component, for displaying them to the user.

The Charting component uses the open-source charting library JFreeChart to graph the KPIs.

Detailed Explanation

We will use a very basic sample workflow definition in the example. This definition is the one used previously on the Hello World section of this chapter. We have modified it to send more events to the engine during its lifespan and to use the event type we talked about in the previous section. The XML definition is as following:

```xml
<?xml version="1.0" encoding="UTF-8"?>
<!DOCTYPE workflow PUBLIC "-//OpenSymphony Group//DTD OSWorkflow 2.6//
EN" "http://www.opensymphony.com/osworkflow/workflow_2_8.dtd">
<workflow>
  <initial-actions>
    <action id="100" name="Start Workflow">
      <post-functions>
        <function type="class">
          <arg name="class.name">
            packtpub.osw.cep.PushEventFunctionProvider
          </arg>
          <arg name="event.class.name">
            packtpub.osw.cep.ex1.ProcessCreationEvent
          </arg>
        </function>
      </post-functions>
      <results>
        <unconditional-result old-status="Finished" status="Underway"
                                                    step="1" />
      </results>
    </action>
  </initial-actions>
  <steps>
    <step id="1" name="Sending event">
      <actions>
        <action id="1" name="Finish First Draft">
          <results>
            <unconditional-result old-status="Finished"
                                      step="2" status="Underway">
              <post-functions>
                <function type="class">
                <arg name="class.name">
                        packtpub.osw.cep.PushEventFunctionProvider
```

```
          </arg>
          <arg name="event.class.name">
                packtpub.osw.cep.ex1.ProcessFailureEvent
          </arg>
          </function>
        </post-functions>
      </unconditional-result>
    </results>
   </action>
  </actions>
</step>
<step id="2" name="Edit Doc">
  <post-functions>
    <function type="class">
    <arg name="class.name">
                    packtpub.osw.cep.PushEventFunctionProvider
    </arg>
    <arg name="event.class.name">
                    packtpub.osw.cep.ex1.ProcessCompletionEvent
    </arg>
    </function>
  </post-functions>
</step>
</steps>
</workflow>
```

This definition uses the `FunctionProvider` to send events to Esper as soon as it is created (`ProcessCreationEvent`), a sample `ProcessFailureEvent` on the completion of the first step, and a `ProcessCompletionEvent` when it finishes. This allows us to test all three events.

The EQL queries that make up the KPIs are as follows:

```
select 'creation' as name,count(*) as value from packtpub.osw.cep.ex1.
ProcessCreationEvent.win:time(1 minutes)

select 'completion' as name,count(*) as value from packtpub.osw.cep.
ex1.ProcessCompletionEvent.win:time(1 minutes)

select 'failure' as name,count(*) as value from packtpub.osw.cep.ex1.
ProcessFailureEvent.win:time(1 minutes)
```

The three EQL queries are essentially the same, calculating how many events of each type were processed each minute. Finally, the `GraphListener` code is as follows:

```
package packtpub.osw.cep.ex1;

import java.util.ArrayList;
import java.util.Date;
```

```java
import java.util.List;
import java.util.Map;

import net.esper.client.UpdateListener;
import net.esper.event.EventBean;

/**
 * Simple listener that prints the event to console.
 */
public class GraphListener implements UpdateListener
{
  public static List graphValues = new ArrayList(50);
  public void update(EventBean[] newEvent, EventBean[] oldEvent)
  {
    for (int i = 0; i < newEvent.length; i++)
    {
      EventBean bean = newEvent[i];
      Map eventMap = (Map)bean.getUnderlying();
      GraphData gd = new GraphData(new Date(),
                                   (Long)eventMap.get("value"),
                                   (String)eventMap.get("name"));
      if(graphValues.size() > 50)
      {
        synchronized (graphValues)
        {
          System.out.println("removing");
          graphValues.remove(0);
        }
      }
    graphValues.add(gd);
    }
  }
}

class GraphData
{
  private Date timestamp;
  private double value;
  private String category;
  /**
   * Constructor.
   * @param timestamp
   * @param value
   * @param category
   */
  GraphData(Date timestamp, double value, String category)
  {
    super();
```

```
      this.timestamp = timestamp;
      this.value = value;
      this.category = category;
   }
   /**
    * @return the category
    */
   public String getCategory()
   {
      return category;
   }
   /**
    * @return the timestamp
    */
   public Date getTimestamp()
   {
      return timestamp;
   }
   /**
    * @return the value
    */
   public double getValue()
   {
      return value;
   }
}
```

This `GraphListener` code is invoked when the pattern is matched. It communicates with the charting component through the use of a shared data structure called `graphValues`. The main section of the code is as follows:

```
package packtpub.osw.cep.ex1;

import java.awt.Rectangle;
import java.awt.image.BufferedImage;
import java.util.*;
import javax.swing.*;
import net.esper.client.*;
import org.jfree.chart.*;
import org.jfree.data.time.*;
import com.opensymphony.workflow.Workflow;
import com.opensymphony.workflow.basic.BasicWorkflow;
import com.opensymphony.workflow.config.*;
import packtpub.osw.cep.CEPWorkflowTest;

/**
 * CEP Example1
 */
```

```java
public class Example1
{
  public static void main(String[] args)
  {
    setupEngine();
    Workflow workflow = new BasicWorkflow("test");
    Configuration config = new DefaultConfiguration();
    workflow.setConfiguration(config);
    try
    {
      while(true)
      {
        long workflowId = workflow.initialize("cep-example1", 100,
                                      Collections.EMPTY_MAP);
        workflow.doAction(workflowId, 1, Collections.EMPTY_MAP);
        graph();
      }
    } catch (Exception e)
      {
        e.printStackTrace();
      }
  }

  private static void setupEngine()
  {
    EPServiceProvider epService = EPServiceProviderManager
                                        .getDefaultProvider();
    EPAdministrator admin = epService.getEPAdministrator();
    //creation rate
    EPStatement eq1 = admin.createEQL("select 'creation' as
                                      name,count(*) as value from
                                      packtpub.osw.cep.ex1.
                                      ProcessCreationEvent.win:time
                                      (1 minutes)");
    //completion rate
    EPStatement eql2 = admin.createEQL("select 'completion' as
                                      name,count(*) as value from
                                      packtpub.osw.cep.ex1.
                                      ProcessCompletionEvent.
                                      win:time(1 minutes)");
    //failure rate
    EPStatement eql3 = admin.createEQL("select 'failure' as
                                      name,count(*) as value from
                                      packtpub.osw.cep.ex1.
                                      ProcessFailureEvent.win:time
                                      (1 minutes)");
    GraphListener pl = new GraphListener();
```

```
    eql.addListener(pl);
    eql2.addListener(pl);
    eql3.addListener(pl);
}

private static JFrame jf;
private static JLabel lblChart;

private static void graph()
{
    if (jf == null)
    {
        setupGraphicSubsystem();
    }
    TimeSeriesCollection categoryDataset = setupChartData();
    JFreeChart chart = ChartFactory.createTimeSeriesChart
                       ("Event Chart", // Title "KPIs",
                        // X-Axis label "Number of Event",
                        // Y-Axis label categoryDataset,
                        // Dataset true // Show legend, true, true);
    BufferedImage image = chart.createBufferedImage(500, 300);
    lblChart.setIcon(new ImageIcon(image));
}

private static void setupGraphicSubsystem()
{
    jf = new JFrame();
    jf.setBounds(new Rectangle(600, 400));
    lblChart = new JLabel();
    jf.add(lblChart);
    jf.setDefaultCloseOperation(JFrame.EXIT_ON_CLOSE);
    jf.setVisible(true);
}

private static TimeSeriesCollection setupChartData()
{
    TimeSeriesCollection categoryDataset = new
                                             TimeSeriesCollection();
    TimeSeries tsc = new TimeSeries("Creation", Second.class);
    TimeSeries tsf = new TimeSeries("Failure", Second.class);
    TimeSeries tsp = new TimeSeries("Completion", Second.class);
    categoryDataset.addSeries(tsp);
    categoryDataset.addSeries(tsc);
    categoryDataset.addSeries(tsf);
    for (Iterator iter = GraphListener.graphValues.iterator();
                                             iter.hasNext();)
    {
        GraphData data = (GraphData) iter.next();
```

```
        if (data.getCategory().equalsIgnoreCase("Creation"))
        {
          tsc.addOrUpdate(new Second(data.getTimestamp()),
                                            data.getValue());
        }
        if (data.getCategory().equalsIgnoreCase("Failure"))
        {
          tsf.addOrUpdate(new Second(data.getTimestamp()),
                                            data.getValue());
        }
        if (data.getCategory().equalsIgnoreCase("Completion"))
        {
          tsp.addOrUpdate(new Second(data.getTimestamp()),
                                            data.getValue());
        }
      }
    }
    return categoryDataset;
  }
}
```

The main code first sets up the engine, and then it generates new Workflow instances until the JVM is closed. Every time a new Workflow is created, a new graph with information about the last 50 events is displayed.

This code uses the open-source charting library JFreeChart to create a TimeSeries graph, shown in the following screenshot:

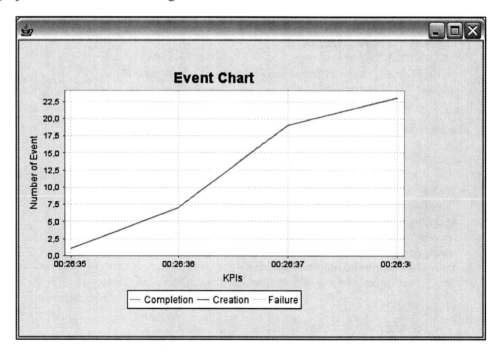

The graph shows the number of events arriving each second (the graph scales automatically).

This example explained the integration between a BPMS and a CEP engine; it can be extended to handle more complex queries. For more information on JFreeChart refer to its website at `http://www.jfree.org/jfreechart/`.

Summary

This chapter covered Esper, a CEP implementation, with BPMS-enabled real-time processing for business process events. The Esper distribution comes with several other examples to evaluate the potential of this new technology.

In the next chapter we'll introduce Pentaho, a very powerful open-source reporting solution, and then we will integrate it with OSWorkflow to generate information charts and reports based on the business process data.

8
Dashboards with Pentaho

This chapter shows how to graphically represent OSWorkflow's business process information by integrating it with the Pentaho open-source Business Intelligence solution. Using the charting capabilities of Pentaho we will build a **Business Activity Monitor (BAM)** dashboard to monitor and analyze the processes.

First we'll integrate Pentaho with the OSWorkflow instance database, giving it access to the business process data, and then by using the Pentaho Design Studio we'll create an `Action Sequence` that will query the database and then graph the results.

What is Pentaho?

Pentaho is an open-source reporting application, with several enterprise capabilities such as chart generation, dashboards, data mining, and pivot table analysis. Pentaho is a 100% Java application, based on the JBOSS application server and JBOSS Portal for advanced user customization of dashboards.

Pentaho also uses several other open-source components, such as:

- JFreeChart for chart generation
- JFreeReport and JasperReport for reporting
- JPivot for pivot table analysis
- Kettle for ETL
- Mondrian as an OLAP server
- Quartz as a job scheduler

By using these products, Pentaho gives a lot of choices for implementation in an enterprise environment.

Pentaho can be used as a standalone application or embedded into your application.

In the following examples, we'll use a standalone option. The integrated distribution includes the Pentaho code and a customized JBoss application server, a JBOSS Portal instance, and a built-in HSQL database. This distribution focuses on ease of use and out-of-the-box experience. To try the distribution, just download, unpack, start the application server, and point the browser to the default page. After completing these steps, you will have a complete, working reporting server.

To create and edit reports, Pentaho uses another industry standard like Eclipse as an IDE for its Pentaho Design Studio. The Pentaho Design Studio provides an easy-to-use environment for generating new reports and Action Sequence components.

The latest Pentaho stable release is 1.2 and the development version is 1.5.2. To learn more about Pentaho and its features refer the website at `www.pentaho.org`.

In this chapter, we'll cover the basics of installing and integrating Pentaho with our OSWorkflow `Workflow` instance database to create graphical charts that help the decision making process as well as the monitoring of business processes.

Pentaho Requirements

Pentaho is a complex Java system, requiring a J2EE application server, thus the memory consumption is huge. If you want to edit the Pentaho components simultaneously, you need to have at least 1 GB of RAM in your system. If you don't have this amount, you'll have to alternate between editing and testing. Pentaho needs at least Java version 5 to run.

Downloading and Installing Pentaho

In this section, we'll download and install both Pentaho and the Pentaho Designer. These two products can be downloaded from the official website at `www.pentaho.org`. A screenshot of the website is as follows:

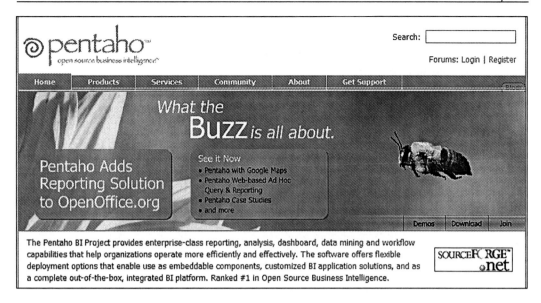

Once the page has finished loading, press the **Download** button at the bottom of the page.

Pentaho comes in two versions—the Stable or GA version and the Development version also called Latest. We'll work with the latest distributions in this chapter. This version has some bug fixes for some of the components we'll work on.

After clicking the **Download** button, the following screen will appear:

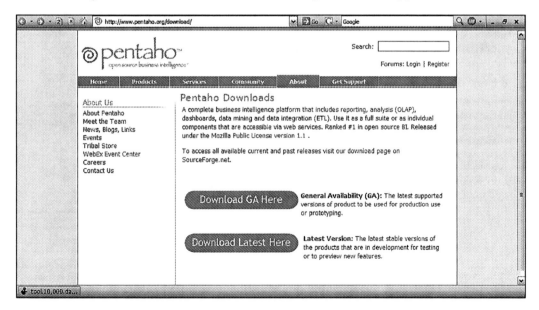

By clicking the **Download Latest Here** button, another page is loaded, displaying all the components available to download. We are interested in the Pentaho BI Demo and the Pentaho Design Editor. After clicking the **Download Latest Here** button, you will see the following screenshot:

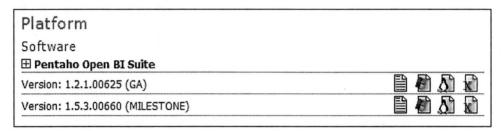

Press your operating system logo next to **Pentaho Open BI Suite** (this is the pre-configured installation) to expand the download box. When the corresponding link is clicked, the site redirects us to SourceForge where the real download begins. The SourceForge web page is displayed in the following screenshot:

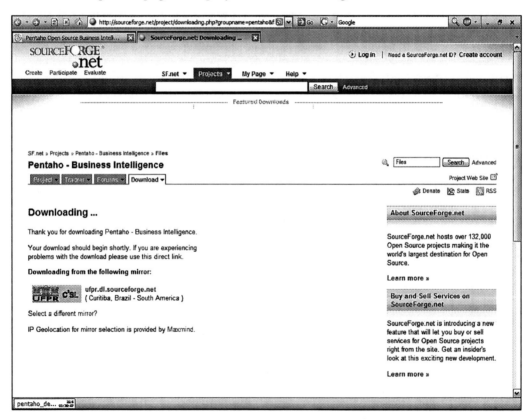

You can change the download location if you wish, as this can sometimes speed up the download process. You'll be asked by the browser where to put the newly downloaded file; it doesn't matter where you put it as long as you remember it. Meanwhile, you can download the other needed software, the Pentaho Design Studio. Go back to the **Pentaho** download page and click on the **Pentaho Design Studio** link; this will open a section in the page where you can chose a distribution suitable for your operating system as shown in the following screenshot:

Select the one for your operating system and you will be again redirected to SourceForge to continue the downloading process. Make sure to write down the download location.

Once downloaded, the two packages must be unpacked. To unpack use any ZIP utility such as the freeware 7-Zip (`http://www.7-zip.org`). When you finish unpacking the files, start Pentaho Server using the following command if you are using Windows:

```
Start-pentaho.bat
```

If you are using a Linux system, then use the following command:

start-pentaho.sh

After you press *Enter*, Pentaho begins the loading phase, starting first its JBoss application server instance. The following screenshot shows the typical output messages:

```
C:\WINDOWS\system32\cmd.exe - run                                          _ □ ×
  JAVA_OPTS:   -Dprogram.name=run.bat -Xms128m -Xmx512m -XX:MaxPermSize=256m -Dsu
n.rmi.dgc.client.gcInterval=3600000 -Dsun.rmi.dgc.server.gcInterval=3600000

  CLASSPATH: C:\pentaho-demo-152\jre\lib\tools.jar;C:\pentaho-demo-152\jboss\bin
\run.jar
===============================================================================
23:28:12,841 INFO  [Server] Starting JBoss (MX MicroKernel)...
23:28:12,841 INFO  [Server] Release ID: JBoss [Zion] 4.0.4.GA (build: CVSTag=JBo
ss_4_0_4_GA date=200605151000)
23:28:12,841 INFO  [Server] Home Dir: C:\pentaho-demo-152\jboss
23:28:12,841 INFO  [Server] Home URL: file:/C:/pentaho-demo-152/jboss/
23:28:12,857 INFO  [Server] Patch URL: null
23:28:12,857 INFO  [Server] Server Name: default
23:28:12,857 INFO  [Server] Server Home Dir: C:\pentaho-demo-152\jboss\server\de
fault
23:28:12,857 INFO  [Server] Server Home URL: file:/C:/pentaho-demo-152/jboss/ser
ver/default/
23:28:12,857 INFO  [Server] Server Log Dir: C:\pentaho-demo-152\jboss\server\def
ault\log
23:28:12,857 INFO  [Server] Server Temp Dir: C:\pentaho-demo-152\jboss\server\de
fault\tmp
23:28:12,857 INFO  [Server] Root Deployment Filename: jboss-service.xml
```

Additionally, Pentaho starts an independent instance of the HSQLDB database for internal usage. It opens it in another command-line window as shown in the following screenshot:

HSQLDB starts and listens for incoming connections to the databases listed in the screenshot. With this, we have got Pentaho up and running; the only thing left is the Pentaho Design Studio. To start the Design Studio, go back to the unpacked directory and type the following command if you are using Windows:

PentahoDesignStudio

If you are using Linux, then type the following command:

./PentahoDesignStudio

This command will open up a splash window while the Pentaho Design Studio loads.

Once loaded, the Pentaho Design Studio looks like the following:

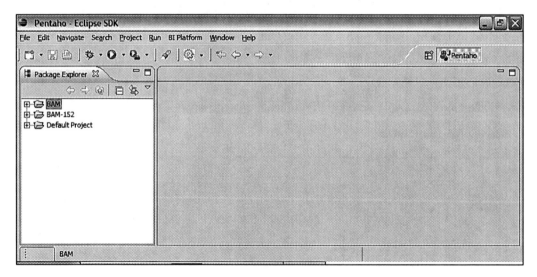

Remember that the Pentaho Design Studio is based on the popular Eclipse IDE, so you can extend it with plugins covering other functionality such as database exploration and editing, application server connectivity, and so on.

Setting up Pentaho to use the OSWorkflow Database

In this section, we will create a bridge between OSWorkflow and Pentaho BI. By using the OSWorkflow Workflow instance database as a data source in Pentaho, we'll have all this process information available for reporting and charting, thereby allowing us to spot trends and monitor the business process visually.

Remember that the Pentaho integrated distribution we downloaded is based on the JBoss application server. Well, this enables us to define a JBoss data source that Pentaho can use to access the OSWorkflow database.

The following XML is the data source definition file for JBoss; the file can have any name as long as it ends with the -ds suffix and has the XML extension. For example, osworkflow-ds.xml is a suitable name. This file must be placed in the deploy directory of the Pentaho JBoss server.

```xml
<?xml version="1.0" encoding="UTF-8"?>
<datasources>
  <local-tx-datasource>
    <jndi-name>solution1</jndi-name>
    <connection-url>jdbc:hsqldb:hsql://localhost/osworkflow
    </connection-url>
    <driver-class>org.hsqldb.jdbcDriver</driver-class>
    <user-name>sa</user-name>
    <password> </password>
  </local-tx-datasource>
</datasources>
```

This XML defines a JNDI name, where Pentaho can look up up this data source to make use of it. This is an important name to remember while using the Pentaho Design Editor.

Also, in this XML file, the URL and the database JDBC driver class have been defined. In this case, we are using the standard HSQLDB JDBC driver and the URL tells the driver to look for a database named osworkflow in the local host.

> At this point, we assume that you are using the HSQLDB database to store the OSWorkflow Workflow instance data. If this is not the case, then just change the JDBC Driver class on the data source and make sure the driver's class is available in the lib directory of the Pentaho JBoss server.

Finally, a user name and password have been defined for accessing the database securely.

This example assumes you have some meaningful data in the `osworkflow` database. If not, use the examples from the Chapters 2 and 3 to fill the database with sample data.

Before we deploy the data source in the JBoss installation included in Pentaho, we must start our own HSQLDB database server. The following command will get it started:

```
java -cp lib\hsqldb.jar org.hsqldb.Server -database.0 osworkflow -
dbname.0 osworkflow
```

Pentaho has a built-in HSQLDB instance that can conflict with your `osworkflow` database instance. You can modify the listening port settings of one of the two servers or you can modify the `start_hypersonic.bat` included in the Pentaho `data` directory. You can also start your `osworkflow` database by appending the following to the Java command line in the file.

```
-database.4 c:/path/to/database/osworkflow -dbname.4 osworkflow
```

This adds another database to the database catalog of the current HSQLDB instance. The first flag points to the file containing the database information and the `dbname` flag sets an alias for the database. This is the alias used in the JDBC URL. If you are using this latest option, you don't need to start the database as the Pentaho startup script does it automatically.

You can download HSQLDB version 1.8 (the one used in Pentaho) from `http://hsqldb.org/`.

The way to start Pentaho is the same as we saw in the last section; just execute `start_pentaho.bat` or `start_pentaho.sh`.

Using the Design Studio to Create our First Chart

In this section, we will create a new Pentaho solution step by step.

Pentaho Design Studio is an IDE based on the popular Eclipse IDE. You can create and test a Pentaho solution from the Design Studio, visually or by editing the `Action Sequence` XML file manually.

`Action Sequence` files are much like a business process; you start with an input and a series of steps to generate content, in our case an HTML report, PDF, or an information chart. `Action Sequence.XML` files describe this process completely with the help of input and outputs.

We will begin by creating a new project in the IDE's workspace. This project will point to the samples included in Pentaho and we will add a new sample. Right-click the left window pane and select **New Project**, and the following dialog box will appear:

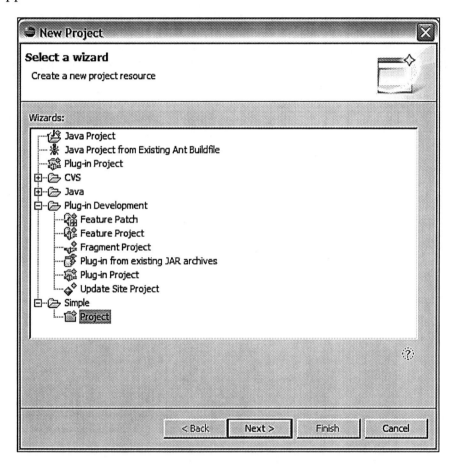

Click on the plus sign of **Simple**, select the leaf node **Project**, and then click the **Next** button to get the following window:

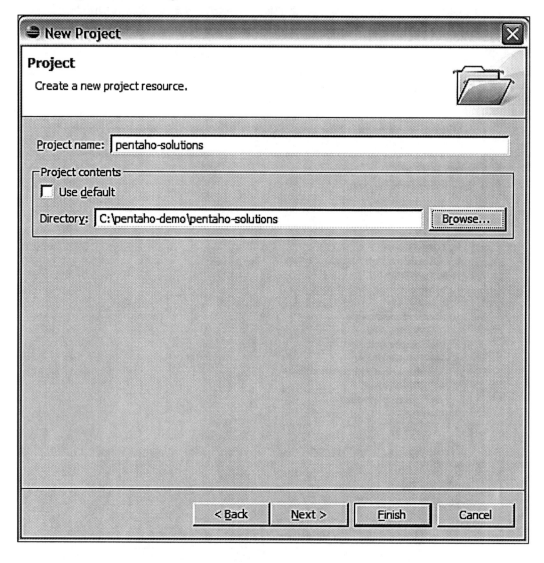

Put the project name you want in the **Project name** textbox, in this case pentaho-solutions, and uncheck the **Use Default** checkbox. The directory of the **Project contents** is the root directory where you unpacked Pentaho suffixed by the directory **pentaho-solutions** in which the Pentaho samples have been stored.

Clicking **Next** will show the following screen, asking for project references. As we don't need to reference any projects, click **Finish**.

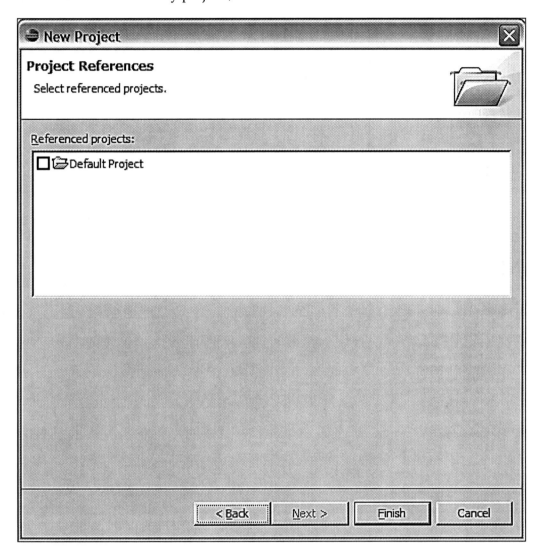

This will create a new project in the workspace with the current contents of the
pentaho-solutions directory.

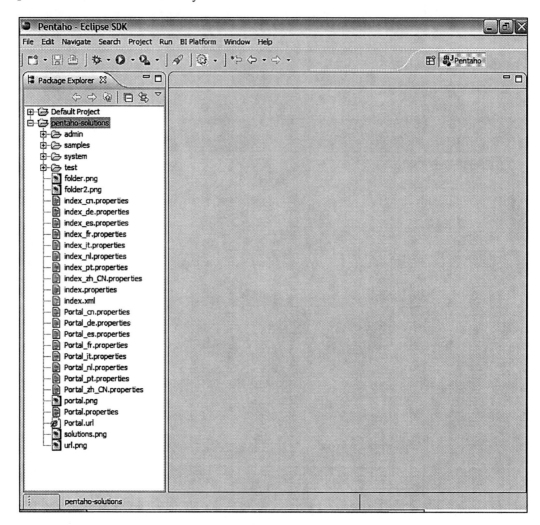

Click on the plus sign to the left of your project's name. Several files and folders should appear. If that's not the case, create a new project and make sure you are choosing the right pentaho directory.

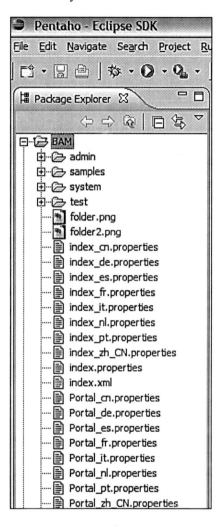

To add our example to the `pentaho-solution`, we begin by creating a new folder. Let's name it BAM for Business Activity Monitoring. To create a folder, right-click the **BAM** project root folder and select **New | Folder**. This will bring up a new dialog box where you can enter the folder name.

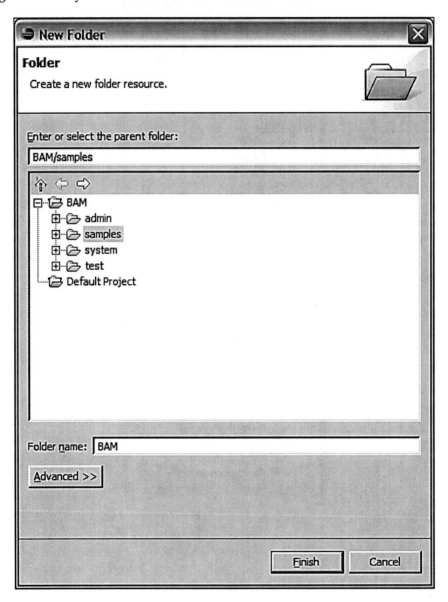

Enter **BAM** in the **Folder name** textbox. After creating the folder, we need to define a new `Action Sequence`. This `Action Sequence` will contain the instructions for generating a graphical chart with the business processes information. To create this `Action Sequence`, right-click the newly generated **BAM** folder and choose **New | Other**. This will open up a **New** dialog box. In this box, choose the **Pentaho** folder, and inside it the **New Action Sequence Wizard**. To proceed, click the **Next** button.

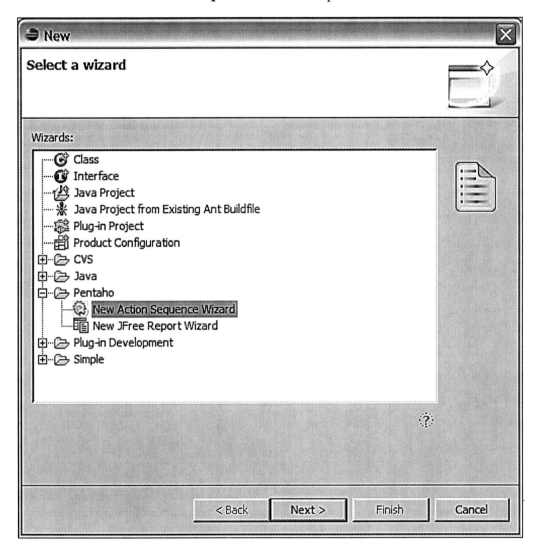

This tells the Eclipse IDE to load and execute the Action Sequence plugin (available as a separate download for existing Eclipse installations on the Pentaho website). The last dialog box asks for a **Container** (a file system folder in this case), a **File name** for the Action Sequence and a **Template** Action Sequence. We'll just name the Action Sequence bam.xaction, but this name can be anything you want.

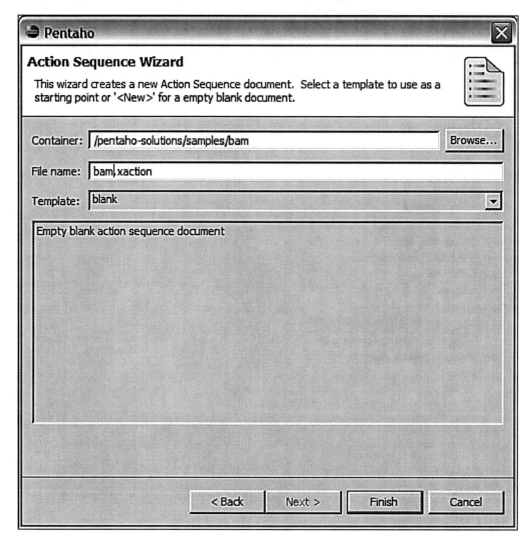

After clicking the **Finish** button, the Pentaho Designer will open the `Action Sequence` file and you will be presented with the following window showing the properties of the `Action Sequence`.

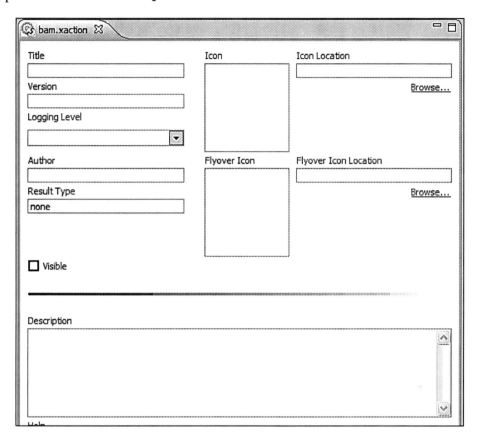

This initial window lets you edit the `Action Sequence`'s general information such as the **Title, Version, Author,** and other administrative data. Fill it up with the relevant information.

You can notice that below the textboxes there are four tabs. We are interested in the **Define Process** tab, which contains a window capable of editing the `Action Sequence` process. The **XML Source** tab allows you to view and edit the raw `Action Sequence`'s XML elements. The **Test** tab allows you to test the `Action Sequence` and see its output in a built-in browser.

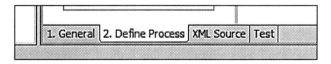

Once you click on the **Define Process** tab, the following window will be displayed:

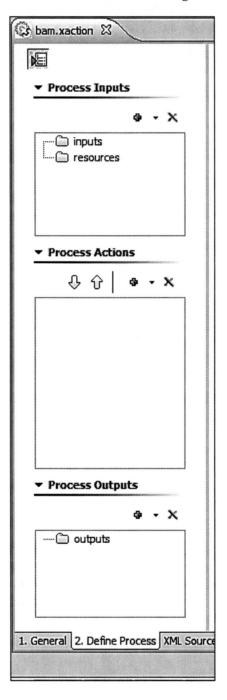

This window allows you to define and edit the **Process Inputs, Process Actions,** and **Process Outputs**. Let's go through each of them in more detail.

- Process Inputs: This is the information that comes from the outside world and feeds the Action Sequence. Another type of process input is a resource that is needed to process the Action Sequence, for example a report template file.

- Process Actions: These are the most important part of the Action Sequence. They define a chain in which each action is executed in the order defined, and the output of one is the input of the next. There are also some conditional actions, much like the while and if programming language constructs.

- Process Outputs: These are the outcomes of the actions and can be the inputs of other Action Sequence files.

To complete our first example chart, we'll add a **Process Action**. Click on the ▾ button and a menu will appear with all the available actions. Select **Get Data From**, and then click on **Relational**. This **Process Action** executes a query on a data source and puts the data available for the next action in the chain as shown in the following screenshot:

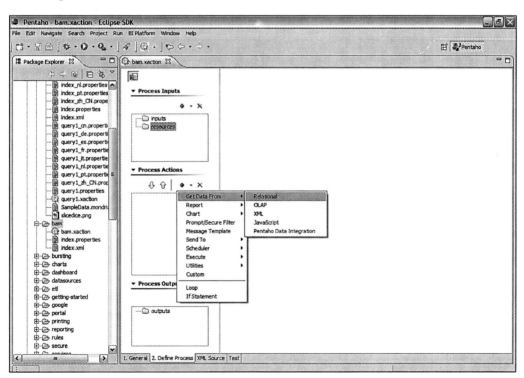

Once you have inserted the new **Relational Process Action,** a new window pane will appear with detailed information about the action as shown in the following screenshot:

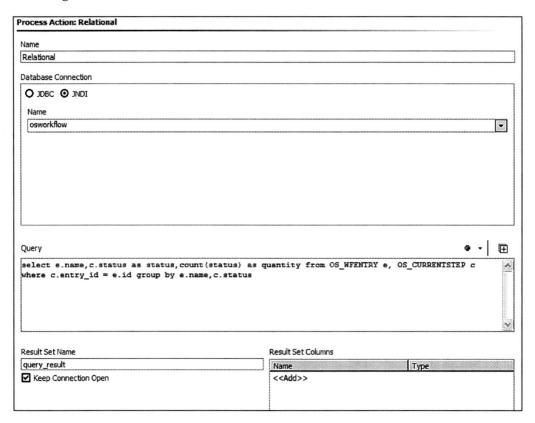

The **Relational Process Action** has several parameters like:

- Database Connection: This enables us to choose the database connection type from **JDBC** and **JNDI**.

- Query: This is the query string to be executed.

- Result Set Name: This is the output of the action. It makes the result of the current action available to the next action in the chain.

- Keep Connection Open: This is a persistent connection option. It is useful for performance purposes if you have to make another query to the same connection in the same Action Sequence.

- Result Set Columns: This refines the name and type of the columns in the output result set.

To complete the example, click the **JNDI** radio button, then type the JNDI name of the data source you deployed in the section called *Setting up Pentaho to use the OSWorkflow Database*. The sample data source that accompanies the book has a JNDI name of **osworkflow**.

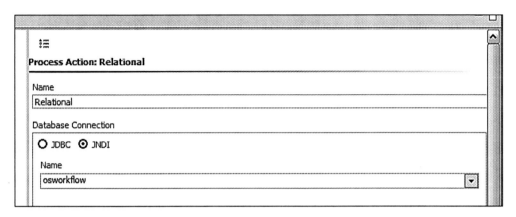

After typing the name, change focus to the query's text field. The first chart that we will implement is one that groups workflow instance data with the corresponding workflow process type and sums up all of them. To obtain a result set that gives us this data, we must type the following SQL into the query's text field:

```
select name,count(name) as quantity from OS_WFENTRY group by name
```

This SQL runs over the OS_WFENTRY (OSWorkflow's master instance table) table, grouping it by the **Name** (this **Name** means the name of the process type) column and counting the instance total by type of process. This **Relational Action** puts the query result set in the variable name defined in the **Result Set Name** text field. By default it has a name of **<query_result>**; leave it this way.

Following the example, we must add a Chart Action to get the result set and create a graphic chart with this data. Click another time on the ✱ icon, select **Chart**, and then **Bar Chart** as shown in the following screenshot:

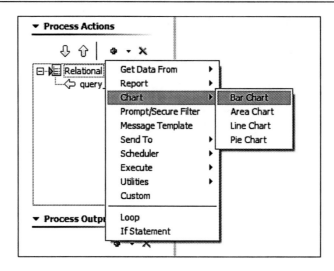

After clicking on **Bar Chart**, the familiar detailed information pane for the Action appears as shown in the following screenshot:

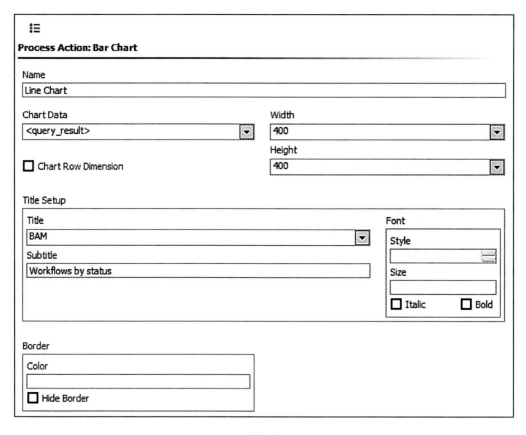

As the result set passes to the next Action in the chain, the **Chart Action** parameter panel has a **Chart Data** field where you can define the result set variable name to graph. In this case it is **<query_result>**. Other parameters you would wish to set are the **Width** and **Height** parameters—**400** is a good number for both, but experiment with the right size for your needs.

Fill the **Title** and **Subtitle** text fields with the **BAM** and "Count by process type". To finish the Chart component switch to the **Process View** by clicking on the uppermost button on the window.

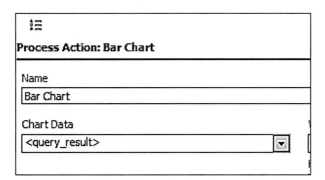

This will significantly change the detailed information pane window. We must set a new output parameter for the Chart component called **image-tag**. This will tell **ViewAction**, the one Pentaho uses to process other `Action Sequence` files, that this is an HTML `image-tag` on the HTML to be displayed. This can be done by clicking on the **<<Add>>** label.

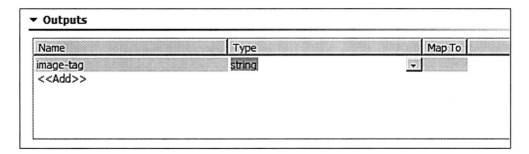

We are done with the **Process Actions**, now it's the **Process Outputs** turn. We want a chart to appear on a web page on the Pentaho BI server, thus the chart must be sent in HTML.

Press the ▾ button of the **Process Outputs** screen and select **image-tag**.

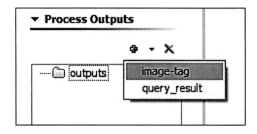

This tells Pentaho that the output of the `Action Sequence` is an HTML `image-tag` pointing to the chart. The `Action Sequence` XML is as follows:

```xml
<?xml version="1.0" encoding="UTF-8"?>
<action-sequence>
  <title>BAM Chart</title>
  <version>1</version>
  <logging-level>DEBUG</logging-level>
  <documentation>
    <author>Diego Naya</author>
    <description>Empty blank action sequence document</description>
    <help/>
    <result-type/>
    <icon/>
  </documentation>

  <inputs>
    <output-type type="string">
      <sources>
        <request>output-type</request>
      </sources>
      <default-value><![CDATA[png]]></default-value>
    </output-type>
  </inputs>

  <outputs>
    <image-tag type="content">
      <destinations>
        <response>content</response>
      </destinations>
    </image-tag>
  </outputs>

  <resources/>
```

```
<actions>
  <action-definition>
    <component-name>SQLLookupRule</component-name>
    <action-type>Relational</action-type>
    <action-outputs>
      <query-result type="result-set" mapping="query_result"/>
    </action-outputs>
    <component-definition>
      <jndi><![CDATA[OSWorkflow]]></jndi>
      <live><![CDATA[true]]></live>
      <query><![CDATA[select name,count(name) as cantidad from
                         OS_WFENTRY group by name]]></query>
    </component-definition>
  </action-definition>

  <action-definition>
    <component-name>ChartComponent</component-name>
    <action-type>Line Chart</action-type>
    <action-inputs>
      <chart-data type="result-set" mapping="query_result"/>
      <output-type type="string"/>
    </action-inputs>
    <action-outputs>
      <image-tag type="string"/>
    </action-outputs>
    <component-definition>
      <chart-attributes>
        <chart-type>BarChart</chart-type>
        <subtitle><![CDATA[Workflows by type]]></subtitle>
      </chart-attributes>
      <by-row>false</by-row>
      <title><![CDATA[BAM]]></title>
      <width><![CDATA[400]]></width>
      <height><![CDATA[400]]></height>
    </component-definition>
  </action-definition>
  </actions>
</action-sequence>
```

From the XML you can identify the inputs, actions, and outputs, and it is useful only for advanced purposes.

We will now test the chart. The Eclipse Action Editor plugin contains a **Test** tab with an embedded browser to test the visual components.

Clicking on the **Test** tab will show the following screen:

The first thing to check is the Pentaho Server URL, for most cases it is fine, but if the Pentaho BI server is running on another machine or port, change the URL to reflect this.

Then press the **Test Server** button to see if the server is responding. If it is not, start the server as instructed in the *Downloading and Installing Pentaho* section of this chapter. Once the server is responsive, click the **Generate URL** button; this URL points directly to our brand new `Action Sequence`. Finally click the **Run** button to see the resulting chart in the embedded web browser.

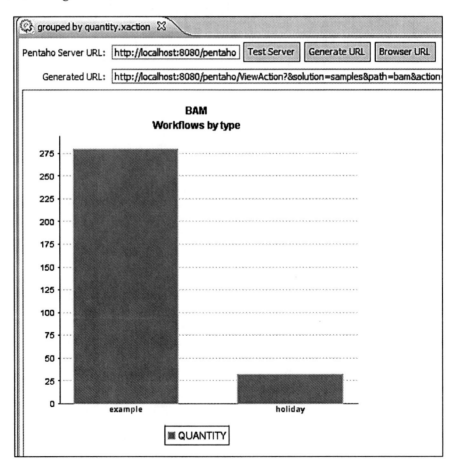

The chart displayed will vary depending on the data you have in the OSWorkflow database.

As this new `Action Sequence` has been saved in the `pentaho-solutions` directory, it can be made available for use in the **Solutions** web page of the Pentaho Server. To register this folder as a solution folder, you must create an `index.xml` file inside the BAM folder with the following content:

```
<index>
  name>BAM</name>
  <description>BAM Charts</description>
  <visible>true</visible>
  <display-type>list</display-type>
</index>
```

Once you create the `index.xml` file inside the BAM folder, enter the **Solutions** page, go to the main Pentaho BI server page (usually `http://localhost:8080/` if you haven't changed the port and Pentaho is running on your computer), then put the mouse cursor over the **Go** menu, and click on the **Solutions** menu item as shown in the following screenshot:

This will open the Pentaho Solutions page with our solution having the name:

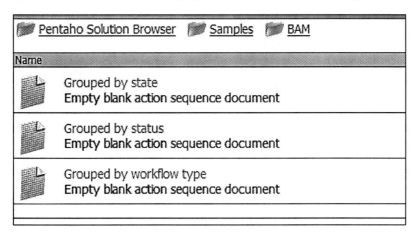

Useful Charts for BAM Consoles

BAM Consoles typically aggregate several charts to inspect the state of the business process from various viewpoints. The chart that we produced earlier depicts the number of business process instances per business process.

The following charts are in demand:

- Number of instances grouped by business process and state (states are: Active, Killed, Completed, etc.)

- Number of instances grouped by business process and status (that is; the current step status)

The first one would graphically be like this:

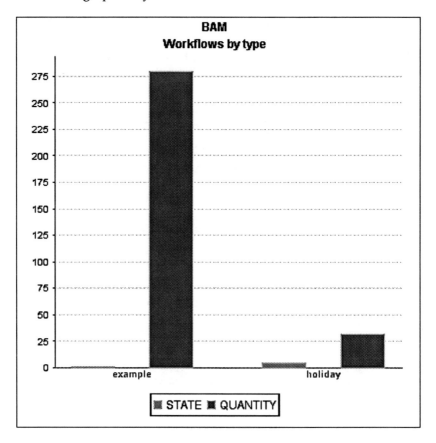

The SQL for generating the chart is as follows:

```
select name,state,count(state) as quantity from OS_WFENTRY group by
state,name;
```

It simply groups the instances into business process and state using only the
OS_WFENTRY table.

The second one would graphically look like this:

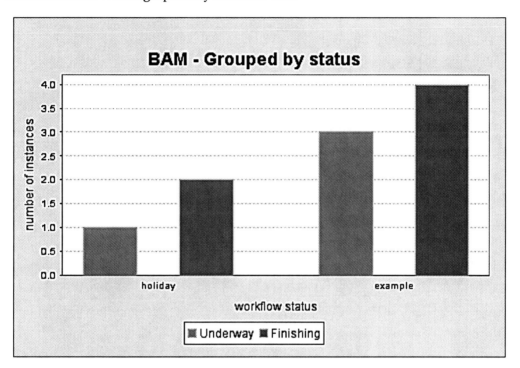

The SQL for generating the chart is as follows:

```
select e.name,c.status as status,count(status) as quantity from
OS_WFENTRY e, OS_CURRENTSTEP c where c.entry_id = e.id group by
e.name,c.status;
```

This query is a little more complex because it involves a join between the master
instance data (OS_WFENTRY) and the step information of every instance
(OS_CURRENTSTEP).

You may probably think of hundreds of other charts to display the information
and might want to use a portal solution to aggregate the charts into one page
of information.

Summary

This chapter covered the integration of Pentaho Design Studio with the OSWorkflow instance database to create Action Sequence files to query and graph the results. As you have seen in this chapter, the Pentaho BI open-source project allows for many useful ways to leverage the business process information visually.

Finally we have completed a whole range of OSWorkflow integrations with other open-source Java projects such as:

- JBoss Rules: Rule Engine
- Quartz: Job Scheduling
- Esper: Event Stream Processor
- Pentaho: Business Activity Monitoring

These integrations enable you to create fully open-source and feature-complete BPM solutions.

Index

sample orchestrator 14

T

trigger functions, OSWorkflow
about 116
definition 116

V

validator, OSWorkflow
about 65
BeanShell validator 66
creating 66
visual process modelling
about 43
end result 47
holiday example, creating 43-46

W

WfMC 17. *See* **Workflow Management
          Coalition**
workflow, security
actions, restricting 94, 95
OSUser 95
step ownership 95
step permissions 93, 94
user and group authentication, extending
          95
workflow, unit testing
about 82
JUnit 82
JUnit, TestCase 82-85
TestRunner 85
tests, running 85
workflow building blocks
about 29-33
splits and joints 34, 35, 37
workflow definition, testing 33
workflow definition snippet 30
Workflow Management Coalition
about 17
architectural model 18

X

XML OSWorkflow process definition
adding functionality 56
BeanShell scripting 60
BeanShell validators 66, 67
built-in functions 60, 61
condition 61, 62
condition, creating 62-64
custom FunctionProvider 58, 59
FunctionProvider 56
FunctionProvider, creating 56-58
FunctionProvider, types 58
LogRegister, using 64
Register 64
Register, implementing 65
validator 65
validator, creating 66

Packt Open Source Project Royalties

When we sell a book written on an Open Source project, we pay a royalty directly to that project. Therefore by purchasing OSWorkflow, Packt will have given some of the money received to the OSWorkflow project.

In the long term, we see ourselves and you—customers and readers of our books—as part of the Open Source ecosystem, providing sustainable revenue for the projects we publish on. Our aim at Packt is to establish publishing royalties as an essential part of the service and support a business model that sustains Open Source.

If you're working with an Open Source project that you would like us to publish on, and subsequently pay royalties to, please get in touch with us.

Writing for Packt

We welcome all inquiries from people who are interested in authoring. Book proposals should be sent to authors@packtpub.com. If your book idea is still at an early stage and you would like to discuss it first before writing a formal book proposal, contact us; one of our commissioning editors will get in touch with you.

We're not just looking for published authors; if you have strong technical skills but no writing experience, our experienced editors can help you develop a writing career, or simply get some additional reward for your expertise.

About Packt Publishing

Packt, pronounced 'packed', published its first book "Mastering phpMyAdmin for Effective MySQL Management" in April 2004 and subsequently continued to specialize in publishing highly focused books on specific technologies and solutions.

Our books and publications share the experiences of your fellow IT professionals in adapting and customizing today's systems, applications, and frameworks. Our solution-based books give you the knowledge and power to customize the software and technologies you're using to get the job done. Packt books are more specific and less general than the IT books you have seen in the past. Our unique business model allows us to bring you more focused information, giving you more of what you need to know, and less of what you don't.

Packt is a modern, yet unique publishing company, which focuses on producing quality, cutting-edge books for communities of developers, administrators, and newbies alike. For more information, please visit our website: www.PacktPub.com.

Business Process Execution Language for Web Services 2nd Edition

ISBN: 1-904811-81-7   Paperback: 350 pages

An Architects and Developers Guide to BPEL and BPEL4WS

1. Architecture, syntax, development and composition of Business Processes and Services using BPEL

2. Advanced BPEL features such as compensation, concurrency, links, scopes, events, dynamic partner links, and correlations

3. Oracle BPEL Process Manager and BPEL Designer Microsoft BizTalk Server as a BPEL server

BPEL Cookbook: Best Practices for SOA-based integration and composite applications development

ISBN: 1-904811-33-7   Paperback: 188 pages

Ten practical real-world case studies combining business process management and web services orchestration

1. Real-world BPEL recipes for SOA integration and Composite Application development

2. Combining business process management and web services orchestration

3. Techniques and best practices with downloadable code samples from ten real-world case studies

Please check **www.PacktPub.com** for information on our titles

SOA and WS-BPEL

ISBN: 978-1-847192-70-7   Paperback: 250 pages

Composing Service-Oriented Architecture Solutions with PHP and Open-Source ActiveBPEL

1. Build Web Services with PHP

2. Combine PHP Web Services into orchestrations with WS-BPEL

3. Use better WS-BPEL to enable parallel processing and asynchronous communication

3. Simplify WS-BPEL development with free graphical tool ActiveBPEL Designer

Business Process Management with JBoss jBPM

ISBN: 978-1-847192-36-3   Paperback: 300 pages

Develop business process models for implementation in a business process management system

1. Map your business processes in an efficient, standards-friendly way

2. Use the jBPM toolset to work with business process maps, create a customizable user interface for users to interact with the process, collect process execution data, and integrate with existing systems

3. Set up business rules, assign tasks, work with process variables, automate activities and decisions.

Please check **www.PacktPub.com** for information on our titles

Printed in the United States
88122LV00004B/65-66/A

9 781847 191526